No Kiln, Han...
CLAY PROJECTS

Many thanks to the company, Pébéo,
who provided all the materials used in this book,
and to my editors, Aude and Anne-Lise, who have once
again trusted me with this ambitious project.
Finally, I would like to thank my grandfather, the sculptor
and ceramic artist, Olivier Pettit, for passing
on to me his passion for clay.

No Kiln, Handbuilding
CLAY PROJECTS

50 ELEGANT PROJECTS TO MAKE FOR THE HOME

CHARLOTTE VANNIER

FOX CHAPEL
PUBLISHING

To learn more about the other great books from Fox Chapel Publishing,
or to find a retailer near you, call toll-free 800-457-9112
or visit us at *www.FoxChapelPublishing.com*.

We are always looking for talented authors.
To submit an idea, please send a brief inquiry to
acquisitions@foxchapelpublishing.com.

Printed in China
First printing

PREFACE

Now more than ever, ceramics and pottery are back in the spotlight and are becoming popular amongst a wide group of people. Perceived as being obsolete for a while, these ancestral arts, practiced by our Neolithic forefathers, are now dominating both designers' studios and our homes. Terracotta charms us with its handmade appearance and poetic imperfections. This material's ability to produce unique pieces is also appealing—it is a return to the slow life, where people take the time to make what they need or want and move away from the trend of industrial consumption.

Excessive industrialization is creating a desire for many consumers to return to their roots. They bake their own bread, create a vegetable garden on their balcony, and make their own pottery. Ceramic and pottery workshops are springing up in major cities to the delight of novices wishing to learn how to work with clay. The saying "take your time" has never had as much value as it does today. In a world that moves faster every day, many people are seeking or rediscovering activities that are soothing, safe, environmentally friendly, and rewarding. This activity, which some people call "hand yoga," has an anti-stress effect, similar to yoga or knitting. Our minds are captivated by the movements and our inner restlessness is quieted. And while we are plunging our hands into the clay, our creativity is in full swing, allowing pottery and ceramics designs that are as unique as they are dreamlike to emerge from the material. Restoring meaning to our dematerialized world is another quest pursued by "neo-potters" and makers who bring traditional craft techniques back to life. Avoiding the use of polluting materials and favoring natural, ecological ones, moving away from mass industry, and going back to traditional jobs to take control of what we consume (i.e., the origin, the composition, or the ethical/non-ethical manufacturing method), are the main motivating factors of the handmade movement, and, in fact, of this pottery revival. We are refocusing on the essentials, the Earth, and especially using the Earth as material.

While pottery appeals to a large number of people, actually doing it can sometimes seem difficult. Even if many centers for novice potters have opened their doors over the past few years, not everyone is lucky enough to have a studio where they can take classes or simply fire their clay creations near their home. Since the pieces need to be fired at temperatures above 1800°F, this can't be done in a domestic oven. Moreover, the requirement for two firings lasting about seven hours (depending on the size of the piece) and a cooling time of about 24 hours between each one, is enough to discourage beginners. Additionally, although essential, a pottery kiln is expensive and takes up a lot of space, plus your electrical system may not be adequate. This is why certain workshops or professional potters rent out their kilns to individuals at reasonable prices that are much cheaper than the cost of buying a pottery kiln.

In order to overcome the issue of firing, clay manufacturers have now created self-hardening compounds that can be worked like traditional clay, but air-dry over a few days through the action of a binder that's incorporated into the compound. The kneading and drying process allow the pieces to harden the same way as a professional kiln.

There are many other advantages to this material. Easy to find and use at home, self-hardening clay allows you to begin learning pottery and ceramics techniques independently. In addition, since the material isn't fired and has a low rate of shrinkage, there's little chance of your pieces cracking, warping, or breaking due to air bubbles, as can happen during firing. It's easy to model and paint, and it's very forgiving of mistakes. Another important advantage of this material is the potential to incorporate other materials like metal, sand, or wood, since the pieces will not be fired at high temperatures.

Self-hardening clay does, however, have its disadvantages. Since the pieces aren't fired and enameled at high temperatures, they're not waterproof. You will need to use acrylic varnishes or paints to protect them, and these can't be used as food containers. Thus, all your creations must be purely decorative. However, there are still many different uses, and even if you make things like dishes, bowls or cups, which are naturally intended for use with food, there's nothing to stop you from displaying them and making them decorative objects in their own right. Trinket trays, vases, and candle or tea light holders are particularly well suited to this technique.

The other consideration to face in making pottery and ceramics is the wheel. While there are some affordable ones, you may not have the space to install a wheel in your home. With this in mind, this book will show you how to make unique pieces using traditional handbuilding techniques, like pinching, slab-building, coiling, or press molding, although throwing is also possible with this type of clay. You will quickly and easily master the first stages of making pottery and ceramics by following the various step-by-step instructions before starting to work with traditional clays in a workshop, if you so wish. You'll discover the many features of self-hardening clay and the techniques needed to make successful pieces, as well as the materials you'll need (the same as for firing clay), how to decorate using paint or glaze, how to color the clay before it dries, how to mix different colors to create patterns (terrazzo, for example), or how to add stamps. Because this material is very malleable and offers many different possibilities, be inspired by the creations in this book and adapt them to your personal preferences, needs, and ideas!

While some people might insist that the feel of self-hardening clay isn't the same as traditional clay, working with this material is still amazing and a lot of fun. You'll reconnect with the joy you experienced as a child playing with play dough and plunging your hands into the wet earth to make mud pies. You'll discover how easy it is to work with no-fire clay and the satisfaction of seeing your handiwork gradually develop under your fingers, letting your imagination run free.

You'll take pride in the unique pieces you create, bringing you pleasure, and perhaps also to the people you give them to. With this book in hand, you can become an apprentice potter or ceramicist in your own home with very little equipment. Your kitchen table will do the job nicely. Jump right in and enjoy!

CONTENTS

BEFORE YOU START

POTTERY & CERAMICS VOCABULARY

Assembly: When a piece is made in several parts (bottom, tower, and handle as in the case of a cup, for example), the different elements must be assembled.

Banding wheel: A round surface that turns on a central pivot. It allows you to view your design from all angles (page 18).

Ceramic slip: A slip is made by mixing water with clay (soft, dry, or powdered). With the consistency of fresh cream, it acts as a glue for assembling the different parts. It can be stored in an airtight container.

Clay/cookie cutter: Available in different shapes and sizes, these allow you to cut out shapes in the clay, such as circles, squares, stars, flowers, and more (page 19). You can use special clay cutters, but also cookie cutters used in baking work great too.

Coil: A sausage of soft clay that can be rolled with the flat of the hand. It is used when making pieces using the coiling technique.

Coiling: This technique consists of stacking coils one on top of the other and then joining them together. Coiling is ideal for making large, free-form pieces, or when you don't have a potter's wheel.

Desiccation: The dehydration or drying process.

Gesso: The main ingredients in gesso are calcium carbonate, titanium white pigment, acrylic polymer, and latex. Generally white in color and the same consistency as acrylic paint, it is used to prime a surface before painting. Its use is particularly recommended on unfired clay, as the paint can't adhere to the medium without this primer.

Hatch marks: A series of small intersecting lines, carved or etched into the clay, when assembling different parts of a piece.

Modeling tool: A tool that's equipped with a wooden handle and a sharpened metal ring at each end. Round, oval, square, elongated, or triangular in shape, it allows you to dig into the clay and remove material (page 19).

Pinching: A technique that involves shaping a block or ball of clay by hand through hollowing, pinching, or molding.

Potter's pin tool: With a wooden or metal handle and a long stainless-steel needle, this tool can be used to cut, pierce, or guillotine clay (page 18).

Press molding: This potter's technique uses molds to shape the clay. In traditional ceramics, we use plaster molds onto which we lay a slab or small pieces of clay. During the drying process, or desiccation, the clay takes on the shape of the mold. Press molding can be done either indented (the clay is placed inside the mold) or rounded (the clay is placed on the outside of the mold). In order to facilitate the removal of a clay piece from the mold, place a sheet of printing paper or cling film over the medium. If you're working in the round, remove the clay piece from the mold before it dries so it doesn't break or crack due to shrinkage.

Rib: Made of stainless steel (page 18), wood (page 18), or rubber, a rib is used to polish and smooth the clay. It has a wide, flat surface with either sharp or rounded edges. If you don't have a rib, you can use an old credit card (page 18).

Scoring: To assemble separate parts, fine cross-hatching must be made at their junction points, and then water or slip is applied. The scoring is made using a pointed tool, such as a pin tool, the blade of a knife, or the edge of a stainless-steel spoon.

Shrinkage: The shrinking or decrease in volume of a piece during the drying process. It is caused by evaporation of the water contained in the clay.

Shrinkage rate: This is the percentage of water or moisture lost when a piece dries. It varies between clays, from about 5% in the case of self-hardening clay to about 12% for firing clay.

Silicone brush: With a wooden handle and a silicone tip, it is useful for precisely shaping clay pieces (page 19).

Slab building: This technique allows the production of pieces without using a potter's wheel. The slab is rolled out using wooden batts, making sure the pieces have an even wall thickness. Different parts can be assembled at right angles or following curves.

Stamp roller: A small wooden roller that is used in baking, but also in pottery. Its textured surface allows it to create impressions when rolled on a soft clay slab (page 19).

Throwing: The technique of producing pottery using a potter's wheel.

Wire cutter: Consisting of a solid wire with two small ends, usually made of wood, it is used to cut the blocks of clay (page 19).

Wooden battens: Available in different thicknesses and widths, they are useful when working with slabs. They enable you to maintain a uniform thickness in a clay slab over the entire surface when rolling it out with a rolling pin (page 19).

Wooden sculpting tool: Available in different shapes to adapt to the potter's needs, it is used to shape the clay (page 18).

IN THE WORKSHOP

You don't need a large workshop or even a dedicated area to work with self-hardening clay. The shaping techniques described in this book don't require a potter's wheel. All you need are just a few tools! You also don't need a kiln to dry the clay, so you can easily work on your kitchen table or desk. However, if you want to really get into this technique and make a large number of pieces, you'll need to get a little organized. Also, if you need to take a break from making your pieces and don't want to have to put everything away each time, a small workshop or dedicated area can be helpful.

Additionally, you will need to let your pieces air dry for a certain period of time (several days), and your living room may soon be overrun by your creative thirst! It's true that when we look at photographs of ceramics and pottery workshops, or when we visit one, we feel a particular fascination. Collections of unfinished pottery, blocks of clay waiting to be worked on, oddly shaped tools, clay dust delicately covering the surfaces, and old clay-covered aprons inspire us and bring us a sense of peace—here, people make things with their hands with patience and love!

So, if you're able to dedicate a small part of your home to this technique, it's a plus, but it's not mandatory! Wooden shelves to dry the pieces on, a workbench that's also made of wood and can be washed, a stool, enough space to store your tools and blocks of self-hardening clay, and a water point is all you need! Unlike a traditional potter, you won't need to take any special safety precautions. Indeed, the dust from firing clay can be harmful to your health because of the possible presence of silica, not to mention the glazes that contain lead and the kiln firing, both of which are hazards. Another advantage of no-fire clay is that it's harmless and can even be used by children. It is, however, advisable to fasten your hair back to prevent it from becoming an unwanted part of your creations.

You will also need to clean your work area regularly by dusting and washing it with clean water to ensure it's clean for each new project, especially if you're using different shades of self-hardening clay. Wash your tools thoroughly to preserve them and prolong their life, and protect your clothes from dirt by wearing an apron.

THE RIGHT TOOLS

There are a variety of tools available for working with self-hardening clay; the same as those used for firing clay, but you'll be happy to know that not all of them are necessary. Start with the basic tools while you get used to the techniques and become familiar with them. Later, when your skills have developed and you have discovered which types of objects you want to make and how you want to work with them, you'll then be in a position to judge what type of modeling or sculpting tools work best for you. Indeed, the sizes and characteristics of each tool are different and your own needs will determine which ones you choose.

To begin, invest only in what you really need—a basic kit will do just fine. These are perfect for beginners and generally include a wire cutter, a smoothing sponge, a wooden sculpting tool, a modeling tool, a potter's pin tool, and two ribs, one in wood and one in flexible steel. You will find all these tools on the next page. Add to that a wooden rolling pin (those used in baking work perfectly well) and a banding wheel, which will make coiling and decorating your piece much easier. You can do without it if you don't want to invest too much at the beginning, or you can use a wooden turntable. You will also need wooden battens of different thicknesses to work with clay slabs, as well as a large rough wooden board to protect your work surface and enable you to easily work with the clay without it sticking to the surface.

If you want to mold your pieces around containers, like glasses, for example, you will need sheets of printing or baking paper to wrap them in order to remove them easily, as the clay will stick to the medium. For press molding, you will need to place some standard kitchen cling film between the medium (a plate, for example) and the clay, for the same reason as above. An old credit card can also help you smooth your design when used like a rib. Finally, you will need fine sandpaper (100/120) to rub it down.

As you progress through the techniques, you will also learn about common tools, like kitchen utensils, cookie cutters, wooden picks, silicone brushes, stamp rollers, graters, and more that can help you work with your pieces.

A BASIC KIT

Potter's pin tool.

Wooden sculpting tools.

Wooden rib.

Wooden rolling pin.

BNP PARIBAS

VISA

Old credit card.

Curved stainless steel rib.

Banding wheel.

Brushes.

Modeling tools.

Wooden sticks
and skewers.

Sharp
stainless-steel
knife.

Wooden
battens.

Silicone brushes.

Stamp
rollers.

Clay cutters.

Sponge.

Wire cutter.

DIFFERENT TYPES OF CLAY

Potters and ceramicists generally use different types of firing clay. The most common are low temperature clay, earthenware, stoneware, porcelain, and paperclay, each of which will be chosen based on the technique used, its qualities and defects, and the purpose of the piece. In the case of self-hardening clay, the varieties are much more limited. Their composition varies little from one manufacturer to another, but each one has its own special characteristics, such as texture, shrinkage rate, or malleability. Each brand also has its own colors, the most classic being white, red, black, and gray. However, as its properties are very similar to those of conventional clays, it is possible to work with it in the traditional way. It can be used for modeling, coiling, slab building, press molding, and wheel throwing.

Be careful not to confuse self-hardening clay and polymer clay, as their composition and use are very different. Polymer clay is intended for making small objects that require precision. It's synthetic and has a smooth, plastic-like appearance, unlike self-hardening clay, which is composed of about 90% natural clay mixed with a non-toxic, synthetic binder and has a porous texture like conventional clay. Moreover, unlike self-hardening clay, polymer clay can be baked at 230°F. As far as cold porcelain is concerned, a recipe for making it at home is easily available. It doesn't contain clay and its appearance is similar to that of polymer clay.

In this book, we have chosen to focus only on self-hardening clay, as its uses and properties are fairly numerous. There's nothing stopping you from making your pieces with firing clay if you wish, as the handling and techniques involved are much of the same. You will need to either fire your pieces in a professional kiln or use them exclusively for decorative purposes, as you won't be able to waterproof them by glazing or painting. Additionally, there is a no-fire clay that can either be air-dried like all self-hardening clays or fired in a kiln: SIO-2 PLUS®.

Self-hardening clay is commercially available in a variety of block sizes: 1.1 lb., 2.2 lb., 5 lb., 10 lb., 25 lb., and 50 lb. Start by investing in smaller blocks before investing in 50 lb. of self-hardening clay! If your project requires more than one 1.1 or 2.2 lb. block, you can mix the blocks together. Finally, these instructions don't specify the quantity of clay you need, so you can make the pieces as big or as small as you wish. You can also choose the shade of self-hardening clay you want and let your imagination run wild!

WORKING THE CLAY

The clay needs to be kneaded until it's soft and malleable. This also makes it smooth, so this step is very important in conventional pottery and ceramics, as even the smallest air bubble can cause the piece to crack during firing. Even if this risk is eliminated when using no-fire clay, this step is still important to achieve the best results.

1 Using the wire cutter, cut off the necessary amount of clay for your project and wrap up the unused clay (see page 24). On your workbench, fold the clay block in half and press down with all your strength. For best results, stand up and use your body weight.

2 Turn the block 90° and fold it back on itself again. Press down firmly on the clay once again, stretching it out in front of you.

3 Fold the block in half and press it flat while stretching it.

4 Continue this process, turning the block 90° every other time until the clay has become malleable. Any bubbles should disappear during the kneading process. If you're working with a small amount of clay that fits easily in the palm of your hand, then you can simply knead it between your fingers.

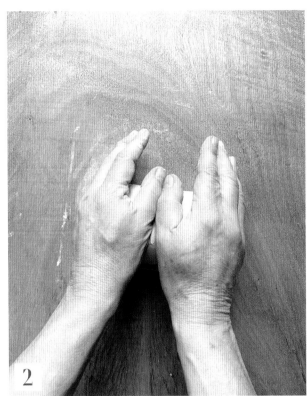

PRESERVING & STORING THE CLAY

As the name suggests, self-hardening clay air-dries at room temperature. You will need to tightly wrap any leftover clay to ensure that it's kept in the best possible condition. You will then be able to use it again later and it will be in the same condition. You should also check the expiry date on the packaging to be certain that the self-hardening clay is still in good condition. Follow this process whenever you take a break from working: wrap your work-in-progress in a damp cloth and cover it with an airtight plastic bag.

1 With the wire cutter, cut off the required amount of clay. Then, wet a tea towel or any piece of cloth—not too thin or too thick—and wring it out.

2 Place your clay block on top and fold the sides of the fabric over the block, covering it completely.

3 Place it in an airtight bag—a freezer bag, for example—and tightly fasten. Protected in this way, your block of clay will be preserved for use at a later date. Store it in a cool place (preferably in the vegetable drawer in your fridge) or in a place where the temperature is between 40° and 68° and away from light.

Note: You can also wrap the remaining clay in cling film, but this is less environmentally friendly.

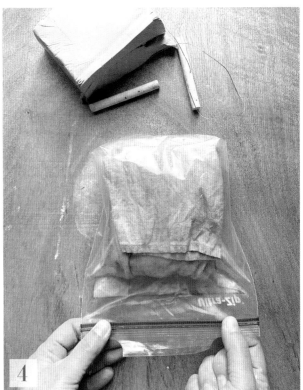

ASSEMBLING THE DIFFERENT PARTS

Some of the pieces you will make, such as the double-arm lamp (see page 28), need to dry a little before being assembled due to their fragility or size. For this type of assembly, don't let the piece dry thoroughly, but resume after about 24 hours when it starts to become more rigid. When assembling a cup handle (see page 32), it's preferable to work with undried clay to ensure a strong joint. As the density and weight of the parts are small, you won't have difficulty assembling them.

Whether you're assembling undried or semi-dried clay, the technique is essentially the same, except with undried clay, you will be making hatch marks in soft clay. With semi-dried clay, your hatch marks will be made in hard clay. These hatch marks are essential to ensure that the different parts don't separate during the drying process. By wetting them or applying slip, these connection points will permanently harden.

Slip is made by gradually adding water to the powdered clay produced by sanding (see page 38) until a clay with the consistency of fresh cream is formed. Store this "glue" in an airtight jar. Add more water, if necessary. You can also make this slip by soaking a piece of dry self-hardening clay in water, or by mixing wet self-hardening clay with a little water added gradually.

Use a sharp knife or a potter's pin tool to make fine hatch marks on the connecting points of the different parts being assembled. After applying water or slip, wait about 20 minutes for it to penetrate well into the hatching and begin activating the fixing process. Then, place small clay coils on the joints and smooth them out with a wooden rib to mask the connection. If necessary, you can polish the joints with a damp sponge.

To prevent handles from warping during drying and to keep them nicely rounded, slide a small piece of rolled paper inside (see opposite page) and place a small wedge underneath. Remove them when it's dry. Finally, polish all the joints once they're dry by sanding them with fine sandpaper (see page 38). This will make all connecting points invisible.

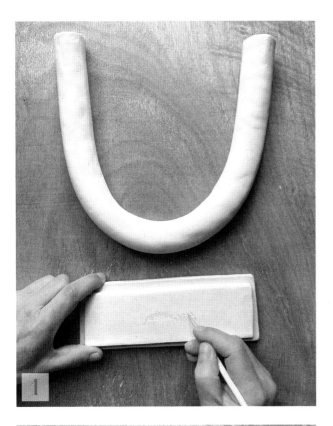

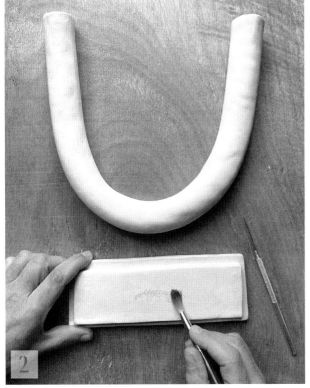

DOUBLE-ARM LAMP

Make a base using the slab technique (see page 98) by placing two different-sized slabs together. Wrap a wooden broom handle with printing paper and cover it with a slab of white clay. Seal the seam and remove the handle from the clay tube. Trim the ends so they are neat and allow the tube to dry in a U-shape. Using a paint brush handle, poke a hole in the center of the U to accommodate an electrical cable when dry.

1 Before the pieces are completely dry, hatch the base slab at the point where it will connect with the U-shaped arms using a potter's pin tool.

2 Remove any clay dust with a brush to ensure solid adhesion. You can store this fine powder in a container and use it later to make slip.

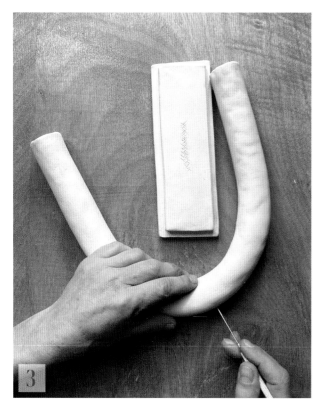
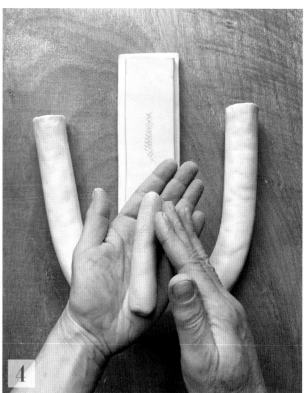
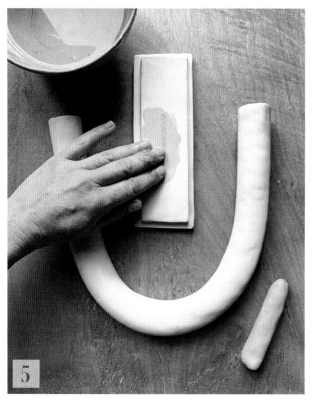
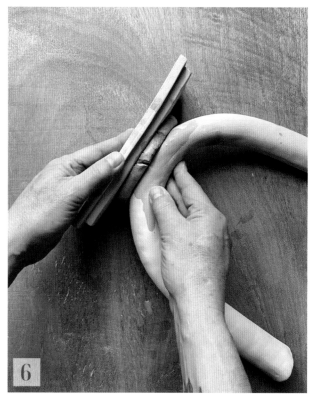

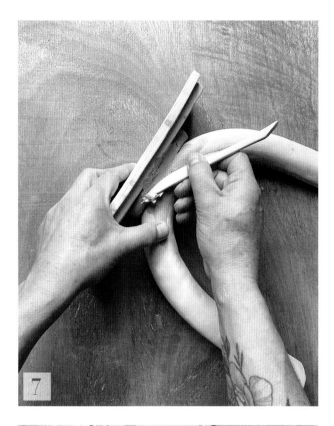

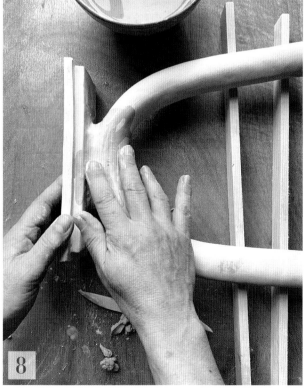

3 With the potter's pin tool, also hatch the underside of the U-arms where they will connect to the base.

4 On your workbench, roll a coil of about 0.6" in diameter and a little longer than the connection point between the arms and the base.

5 Wet the hatch marks on the base and U-shaped arms using your finger or with slip.

6 Place the clay coil between the two parts to be joined and press down firmly.

7 Using a sculpting tool, smooth the coil evenly all around the connection point, overlapping it with the two joined parts.

8 Smooth the connection point with a wet index finger to remove any imperfections.

9 Apply two coats of gesso mixed with baking soda (see page 180), allowing it to dry for 30 minutes between coats. Fit the lamp's electrics.

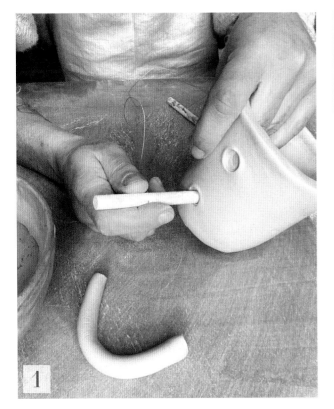

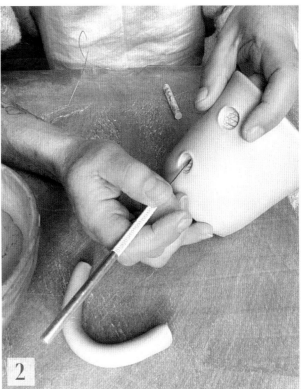

TWO-TONE CUP

1 Make the cup by following the slab building instructions on page 98. Push the tip of the wire cutter into the side of the cup to a depth of 0.08" to 0.12" while making sure not to pierce the cup. If your handle has a larger diameter, enlarge the hole using the tip of the wire cutter by gently rotating it around the center.

2 Hatch the previously made holes, as well as the ends of the handle, using the potter's pin tool.

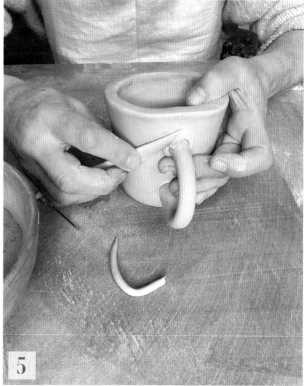

3 Gently push the tips of the handle into the holes on the cup.

4 Roll a thin coil about 0.2" thick on your workbench and wrap it around the two handle connection points. Cut off the excess coil with a knife. Seal the coils using a wooden sculpting tool and smooth them out with a wet finger.

5 To prevent the handle from falling off the cup during drying, and to keep a nicely rounded shape, place a small piece of clay underneath it until it's completely dry. Roll a small piece of paper into a tube and slide it into the handle.

6 Once the piece is dry, apply a coat of gesso and let it dry for 30 minutes. Apply two coats of white acrylic paint, allowing it to dry for 30 minutes between each coat.

7 Paint the handle with gray acrylic paint.

MINI CUP

Follow the same technique for the Two-Tone Cup
on page 32 to make the Mini Cup using
gray self-hardening clay.

DRYING YOUR PIECES

While the clay has great air-drying properties, certain precautions must be taken. To prevent the pieces from cracking, splitting, or warping as they dry, try to achieve an even thickness so they will dry evenly. Smaller pieces will require three to four days to completely dry and be ready for finishing touches, like painting or varnishing. Larger pieces may take up to 10 to 15 days to dry, and depending on their size and thickness, it may even be necessary to slow down the drying process by wrapping them in plastic for a few days to avoid any deformation. Even though the manufacturers' recommendations are for four to five days of drying, consider that this is only a guideline because each piece will vary in weight and volume. Keep these helpful tips in mind and you'll achieve the best possible results as your work dries!

- **Place your wet pieces on wooden boards, a cloth, or newspaper.** In order to achieve optimal drying conditions, as much water as possible contained in the clay needs to be absorbed. Never place your pieces near a heat source (such as a radiator) to try to speed up the process—be patient!
- **Don't place them in a humid area.**
- **Turn your pieces over regularly.** Make sure to move them every two or three days, or more often depending on their size, so they can dry evenly.
- **Change the support if necessary.** The paper, cloth, or wooden board used can quickly become soggy and slow down the drying process.
- **Flat objects might need some weight while drying after a few days.** With flat objects, there's a possibility they may become slightly deformed and lose some of their base. Let them dry for one, two, or three days (depending on their size), then place a cloth or paper on top, along with a weight—something that isn't too heavy, but is suitable for the surface. Then leave to dry again.
- **Check your piece.** To determine if your piece is dry, check the hardness and color on all sides: if parts are a little soft or darker, the piece has not dried completely.

Self-hardening clay has a shrinkage rate of about 5%, while firing clay will have lost up to 12% of its volume when it comes out of the kiln. You should take this into account if you're making a candleholder, for example, by slightly enlarging the hole for the candle so that it can easily fit into its slot after drying. The same is true if you make a hole for a cotton thread, or copper or iron wire. If you need to dry your self-hardening clay pieces in a container that's been used as a "mold," as in the case of press molding, remove it after two days of drying for large pieces and one day for small ones. Don't let the piece dry completely or it may crack. Also, don't cover an object, such as a bottle, without removing it before the clay is completely dry. Finally, place cling film between the "mold" and the clay to facilitate its extraction, as self-hardening clay is more sticky than conventional clay.

PERFECTING YOUR PIECES

The perfecting stage is an important part of the process for creating your self-hardening clay pieces. It's how you achieve the flawless results you expect from your work. Because, even if you have tried to get as perfect a rendering as possible by smoothing the work with a wooden rib, a sponge, your wet fingers, a plastic card, or a stainless-steel rib, there will always be some imperfections. Once your pieces are dry, you'll find it possible to correct certain imperfections. Using sandpaper, you can easily remove small bumps and other minor imperfections like nail marks or small pieces of clay that have accidentally been left behind. Choose a fine sandpaper (100/120) and work as gently as possible.

Sanding also makes the surface perfectly smooth, which is a must if you're looking to remove the rough appearance of dry clay. Moreover, if you intend to enhance the piece by painting or varnishing it, this process will ensure a more uniform application. Sanding will perfect the appearance of the joints on your pieces, like cup handles, for example, that you weren't able to smooth out during assembly. Save the clay powder from the sanding process to use in the glue, or slip, for assembling the parts (see page 26).

If your piece should crack, don't let it dry completely and fill in the gaps with self-hardening clay. Go about it carefully to get a perfect result. If a piece happens to split into two or more parts, which happens only very occasionally, you can reassemble them using a special glue for porcelain, terracotta, stone, and clay (Pattex, for example). It's heat- and water-resistant, dries quickly, and turns white when fully dry. If you used a colored clay, the glue will show and you will then need to paint the piece.

Fill in any gaps (small holes, scratches, etc.) with wet clay or slip applied with a finger or brush. Don't wait until the pieces are completely dry before making these repairs to ensure proper adhesion.

VARNISHING & PROTECTING YOUR PIECES

The main disadvantage of self-hardening clay is certainly its lack of water resistance, as it cannot be fired at high temperatures or have the necessary primers applied to make it impermeable to water and humidity. This is why you must varnish vases, planters, soap dishes, or any container that comes into direct contact with water.

You can also use a special self-hardening clay waterproofing agent that will seal and waterproof your pieces. Based on acrylic resin and fluorescent yellow in color, it becomes transparent and shiny after drying. Marine varnishes, available in matte or gloss finish, are also waterproof and are designed to withstand harsh conditions. By adding more layers, you can create leak-proof containers. In DIY stores, you can also find waterproofing products for terracotta, stone, and brick, which are primarily intended for everyday use in the home.

For a purely aesthetic varnish, a spray one will do the trick. You can find them in DIY craft stores in matte, satin, and glossy.

To keep your pieces in perfect condition over time, clean them with a soft cloth, avoiding cleaning products and water if you've left them untreated. If they're painted or varnished, a damp cloth or sponge will be ideal. Again, don't use any cleaning products, which will alter the colors and varnish. Either way, take care of your pieces and cherish them. The time and effort you've put into making them deserves special treatment!

PINCHING

In addition to being intuitive, the pinching technique is
the simplest in pottery. Ideal for beginners, it requires
very few tools and creates the most original shapes.

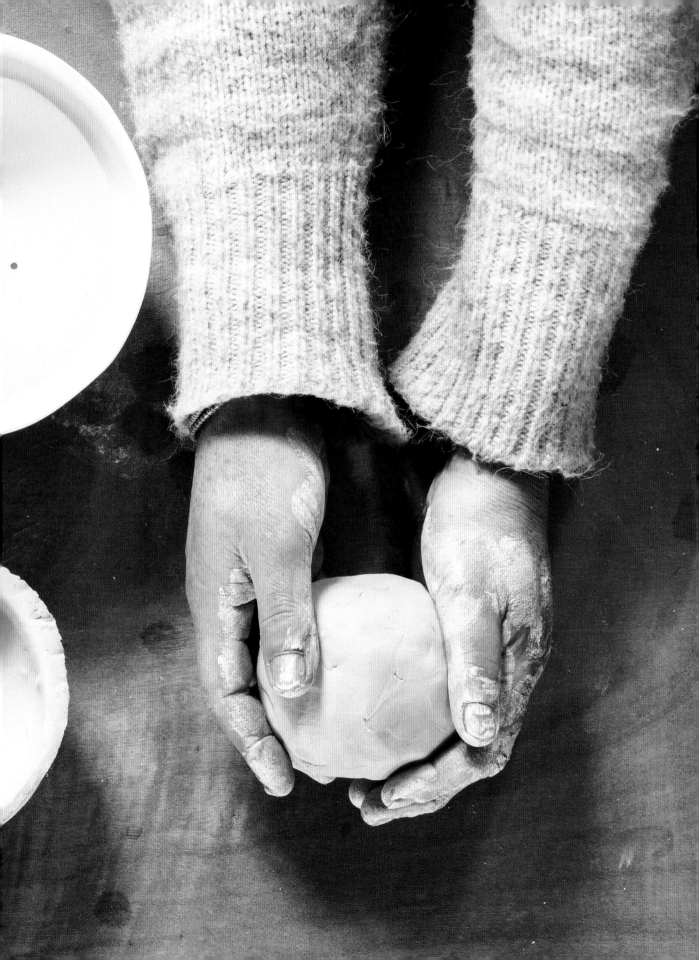

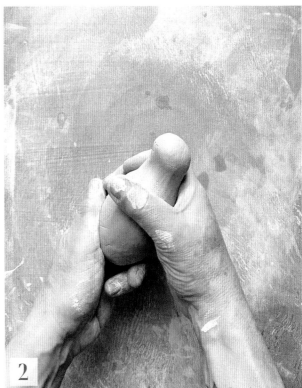

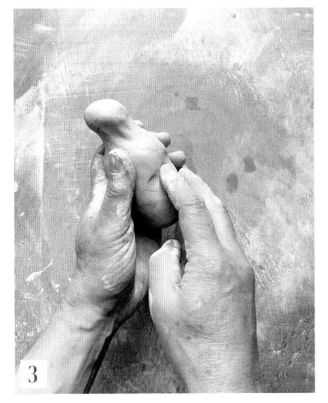

PENGUIN

1 In the palm of your hands, roll a ball of clay into an oblong shape.

2 About a third of the way down, press the clay with your fingers to form the penguin's neck.

3 Two-thirds of the way down, press the clay with your index finger to mark the boundary between the belly and the chest.

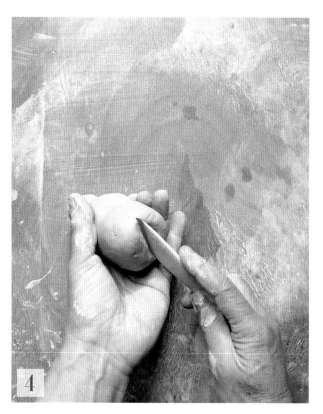

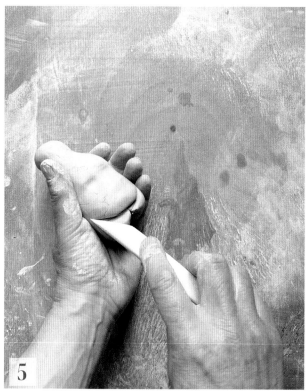

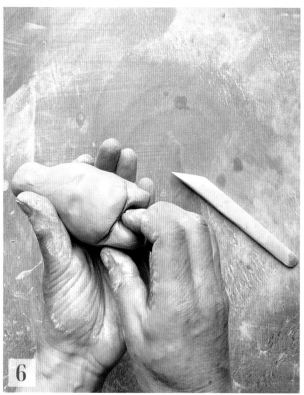

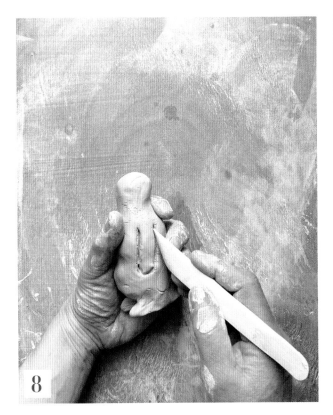

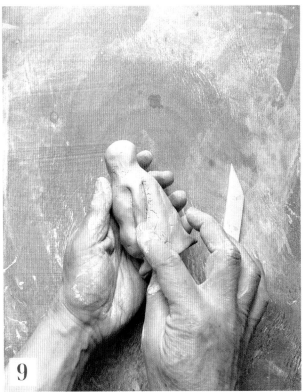

4 With a sculpting tool, mark the underbelly with a line about 0.4" deep and angle the sculpting tool 45° to either side of this line.

5 Lightly mark the rounding of the lower belly by creating an arc with the sculpting tool.

6 Begin pinching the overall shape, starting with the feet. Then shape the lower belly. Pinch the tip of each foot, continuing to work on the rounding of the lower abdomen.

7 Press the heels into a point, then smooth the bottom of the feet using your sculpting tool or finger.

8 With the sculpting tool, trace the curve of the arms on each side of the figure.

9 Shape the size of the arms, following the lines you made earlier. Use your index finger to press on the outside of the lines to make the arms bigger.

10 Work the top of the head by stretching the clay slightly to give it a beak shape.

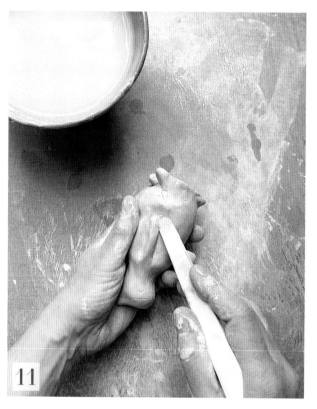

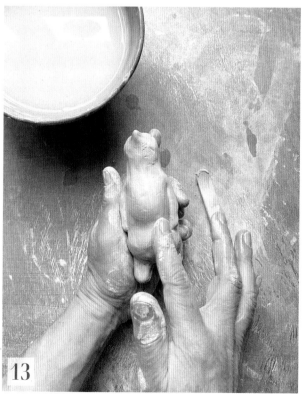

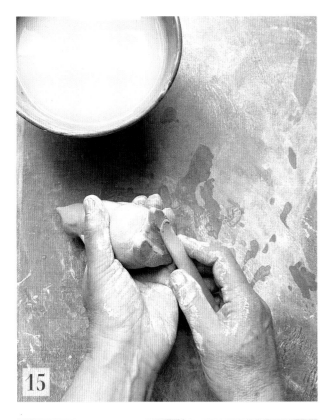

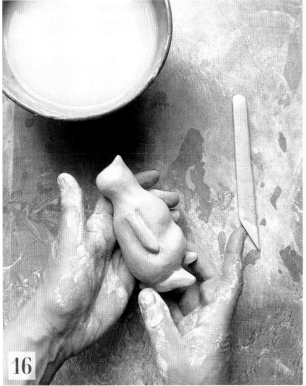

11 With the round, flat tip of the sculpting tool, fine-tune the shaping of the whole piece.

12 Wet the sculpting tool and use its rounded tip to smooth out as many imperfections as possible.

13 Smooth the figure again, this time using a wet finger.

14 Pick up the sculpting tool again and continue shaping the piece to smooth the curves and remove any finger marks.

15 Continue this process on all sides of the figure. If necessary, change sculpting tools or use the tip of the sculpting tool for fine details. If you have them, you can also use silicone brushes to work more precisely. Finish off with the underside of the feet.

16 Gently rotate the piece in your hands and check that all imperfections are gone. Assess the overall shape and rework it slightly if necessary.

17 Once the piece is dry, apply a coat of gesso and allow it to dry for 30 minutes. Then apply two coats of white acrylic paint, letting it dry for 30 minutes between each coat. Using a small brush, paint the beak gold (see page 180).

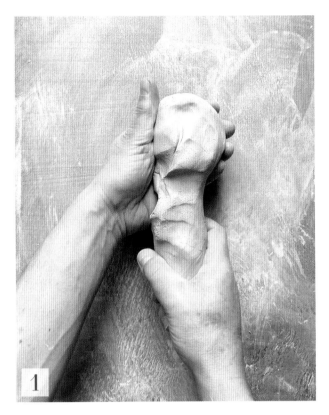

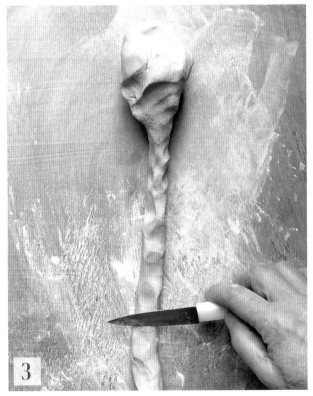

SPOONS

1 In the palm of your hands, roughly shape a sausage, leaving a
ball on top.

2 Refine the sausage to form the handle by pressing lightly
along the length with your curled fingers.

3 Cut off about 4" from the base of the ball. Shape the handle
by rolling it gently on the board like a coil (see page 74).

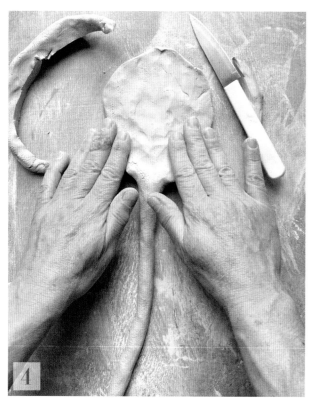

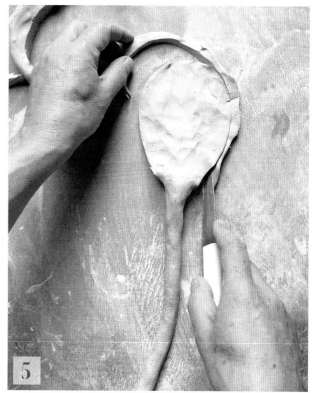

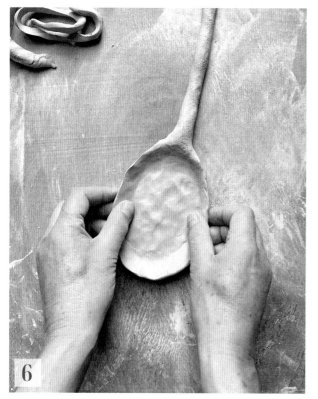

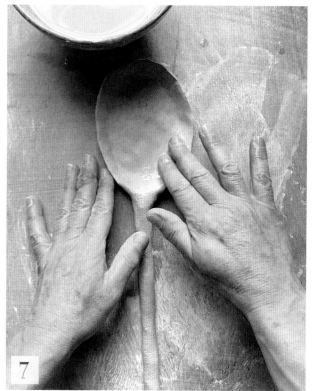

4 Flatten the ball to a thickness of about 0.8" and trim away the edges of the clay.

5 If necessary, flatten it again and cut it more precisely to the desired shape and size.

6 Shape the hollow of the spoon by slightly raising the edges: place your fingers under the spoon and use your thumbs to define the rim and the curvature.

7 Smooth the inside of the spoon with wet fingers and finish the edges.

8 Finish smoothing the spoon, again with wet fingers, then work on the handle and underside.

9 Once the spoons are completely dry, they can be left in their natural state or painted following the steps on page 187.

WREATH

Instructions on page 56.

CANDLE HOLDERS

Instructions on page 58.

WREATH

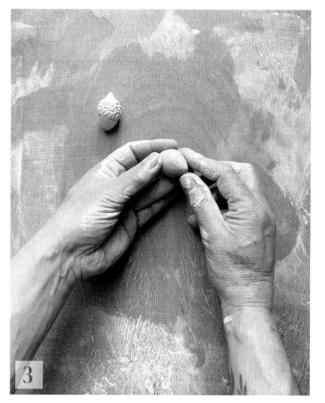

1-3 In the palm of your hands, roll a ball of clay. Carefully stretch it into an oblong shape. Gently taper one side to a point using your fingers.

4 On the other side, shape the hanger by pressing gently with your fingers.

5 Draw a line around the circumference with the sculpting tool and then use the flat side to press along underneath the line. Reshape the lower part with your fingertips.

6 Use a wooden skewer to make a hole through the top of the acorn, about 0.4" from the tip.

7 Use the tip of the skewer to prick around the upper part of the acorn to a depth of 0.04". Make three more acorns in the same way.

8 Shape five oak leaves using the slab technique (see page 98) and mark them using the skewer. Once the piece is dry, apply a coat of gesso and allow it to dry for 30 minutes. Paint the leaves and acorns with gold and white acrylic paint (see page 180). Attach them to a metal ring using thin gold wire.

CANDLE HOLDERS

1 In the palm of your hands, roll a ball of clay into an oblong shape.

2 Place it on your workbench and press down lightly with the flat of your hand to flatten the base.

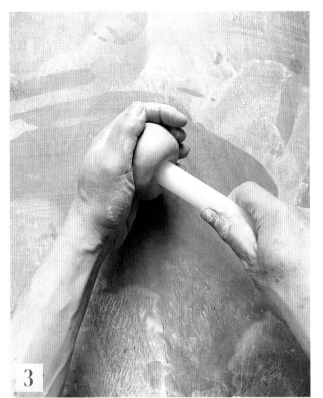

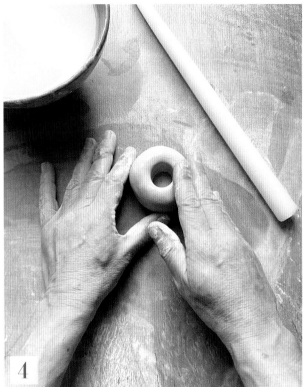

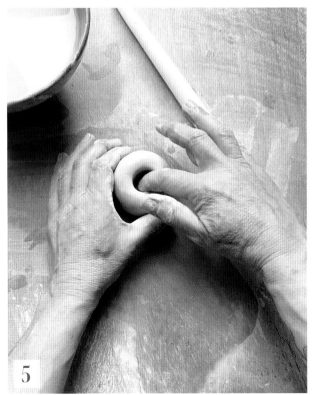

3 Push a candle into the center of the shape on the rounded side. Do this gently to avoid distorting the candle holder, then remove the candle by rotating it slightly so it comes out of the hole easily.

4 Smooth the candle holder on all sides with your wet fingertips.

5 Enlarge the hole using your wet index finger. This is necessary to ensure that the candle will fit into the hole after it has dried completely, as the self-hardening clay shrinks as it dries.

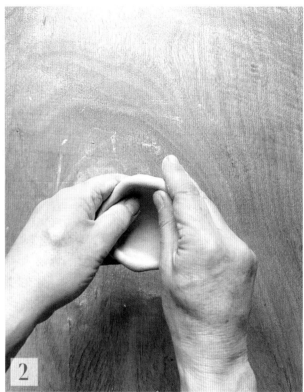

MINI CANDLES

1 In the palm of your hands, roll a ball of clay of about 2-2.5".

2 Hollow out the ball with your fingers to the desired thickness. Ensure an even thickness on all sides and the bottom for optimal drying.

3 Smooth the pot with your wet fingers to remove any imperfections. Starting with the inside, lightly press the entire surface of the pot evenly. Then smooth the underside, and finally, the outside.

4 Once the piece is dry, apply a coat of gesso and allow it to dry for 30 minutes. Apply two coats of white acrylic paint on the top and inside, and sand-colored on the lower part. Allow it to dry for 30 minutes between each coat. Position the candle wicks and fill with liquid wax. Leave to harden.

MINI BELLS

1 Work on the body of the bell following the steps on page 61 Shape the end into a point or leave it rounded. Pierce it with a skewer to make a hole in the center.

2 Roll a small portion of clay into a ball in the palm of your hand.

3 Poke a hole through the ball using the skewer, making sure it's in the center of the ball. If you want to hang multiple beads from your bell, make more in the same way.

4 Once it's completely dry, thread a length of string folded in half through the holes in the bell, leaving the loop on top, then thread both strands through the balls. Fix the bell and balls in place with simple knots.

FLOWER VASE

1 Flatten a ball of clay on your workbench using a rolling pin until it is about 0.4" thick. Use wooden battens, if necessary. Cut out different sized paper flower templates and place them on the clay slab. Trace around them using a potter's pin tool.

2 Cut out the shapes using the potter's pin tool and trim off the excess clay.

3 Shape the petals by working with your fingertips to give them fullness and rounded edges.

4 Using the pointed end of the sculpting tool, make grooves in the center of each petal.

5 Still with the pointed end, tilt the sculpting tool 45° to either side of the grooves.

6 Using a less pointed, moistened sculpting tool, accentuate the grooves and then smooth them out.

7 Gently smooth each petal with a wet index finger and re-contour the shapes as needed. If you have them, use silicone brushes for more precision.

8 Place two large flowers on top of one another with alternating petals, then a smaller one on top. Press down on the center with your index finger to fuse them together.

9 Roll a small ball of clay about 0.4" in diameter in the palm of your hands and place it in the center of the petals. Press it down to attach and flatten it.

10 With the tip of a skewer, make small holes in the flattened ball. Push the tip in to a depth of approximately 0.4" to ensure that all the elements adhere to one another.

11 Once the piece is dry, apply a coat of gesso and allow it to dry for 30 minutes. Apply two coats of acrylic paint, allowing it to dry for 30 minutes between each one (see page 180). Make the vase following the slab building instructions (see page 98), then attach the flower with a dab of special pottery glue.

FLAMING HEART VOTIVE

1 Flatten a ball of clay on your workbench using a rolling pin until it is about 0.8" thick.

2 Trace out the heart and flame shapes using the potter's pin tool and then use it to cut out the traced shape. Discard the excess clay.

3 Using the pointed end of a sculpting tool, make grooves to create the votive's flames.

4 Round off the flames and the heart-shape using the sculpting tool.

5 Cut the clay and smooth it as you go.

6 Press your index finger into the center of the heart to hollow it out and place a ball of clay in the indentation.

7 Roll out a new ball of clay to a thickness of about 0.1" and place the votive on top. Cut around the heart-shape using the potter's pin tool and then set the votive aside.

8 Draw and cut out an eye shape in the center of the heart-shaped slab using the potter's pin tool.

9 Place the two parts on top of each other, making sure the edges are aligned.

10 Press them together so they adhere to each other.

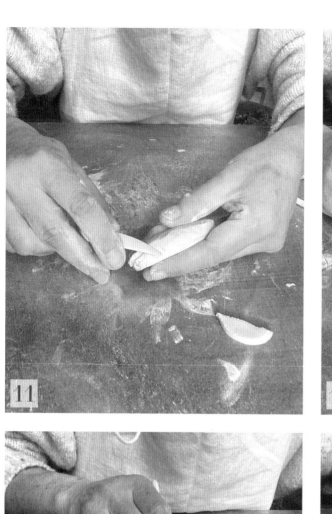

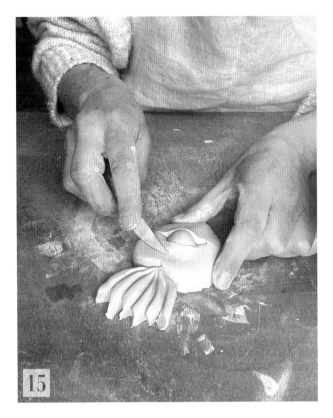

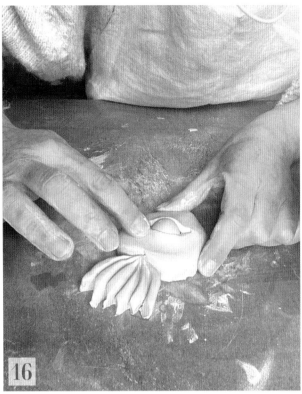

11 Smooth the edges with the sculpting tool to hide where they join.

12 & 13 Shape the flames using a combination of the sculpting tool and your fingers.

14 Smooth the flames with a wet index finger.

15 Smooth the top of the votive using the sculpting tool, paying particular attention to the upper and lower eyelids. Work from the flat area towards the edge of the eyelid to create fullness and bring the eyelid up over the eye. Work gradually and carefully.

16 Smooth over the votive with a wet index finger to remove any imperfections.

17 Reshape the eyelid if necessary, using the pointed end of the sculpting tool. Use silicone brushes for more precision if you have them.

18 Once the piece is dry, apply a coat of gesso and allow it to dry for 30 minutes. Paint the votive using flesh colored, sky-blue, gold, white, and black acrylic paints. Apply two coats, allowing it to dry for 30 minutes between each coat (see page 180).

COILING

Coiling involves forming pieces using clay coils that are stacked on top of each other, then joined and smoothed. While this technique works well without a potter's wheel, a banding wheel is useful for checking all sides of the piece.

CONE VASE

1 Shape the clay into 0.4" thick coils by rolling them out on the workbench. You can make them as you shape the vase, or prepare them in advance and keep them under a damp cloth. Wrap a coil around itself in the center of the banding wheel to form a snail shape. Keep the rows tight.

2 When you have the diameter you want for the base, cut off the excess coil with a knife.

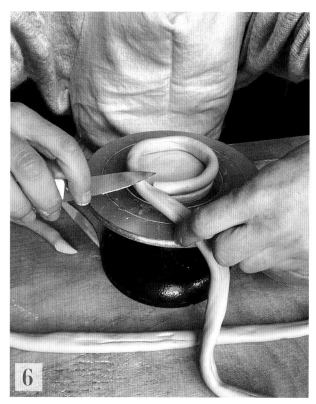

3 Stick the coils together by pinching them with your thumb and forefinger, then stretching them from outside to inside with your finger.

4 Use the sculpting tool to smooth out the clay disc completely. Start from the outside and work your way to the center, then smooth out the whole thing. Turn the clay disc over and do the same on the other side.

5 Smooth both sides of the disc thoroughly using a steel scraper or a used credit card.

6 Place a first coil around the edge of the clay disc and cut off the excess with a knife.

7 Join the two ends of the coil by applying pressure with your fingers.

8 Place a second coil of the same length over the first and join its ends in the same way.

13

14

9 With the flat part of the sculpting tool's pointed end, join the outer seams from the bottom of the piece to the top.

10 Using a round-ended sculpting tool, smooth the coil seams on the inside of the vase.

11 & 12 Place two new rows of coils on top of the piece, gradually decreasing their length to narrow the neck of the vase.

13 As described in step #9, join the outside edges with the flat part of the sculpting tool's pointed end, starting from the bottom of the piece and working up.

14 As described in step #10, smooth the coils on the inside of the vase using a round-ended sculpting tool.

15 & 16 Place two new rows of coils on top of the whole, gradually decreasing their length once again.

17 Place a final coil (or two more, depending on the height of the neck you want) over the opening, then join and smooth it out as you did the previous ones.

18 Smooth the full length of the vase using a wet sculpting tool. You can also use a wooden rib or steel scraper, also dipped in water.

19 Smooth the vase thoroughly with your wet hands while turning it on the banding wheel. Check all sides of the vase, as well as the alignment of the neck. If it's not completely centered, place your hands flat on either side of the vase and straighten it slightly.

20 Smooth the inside of the vase at the neck using a wet index finger.

21 Once the piece is dry, apply a coat of gesso and allow it to dry for 30 minutes. Apply two coats of white acrylic paint, allowing it to dry for 30 minutes between each coat (see page 180).

RAINDROP VASE

Using the same technique as the Cone Vase on page 76, make this Raindrop Vase out of black self-hardening clay, then varnish once it's dry (see page 40).

BUD VASE

Using the same technique as the Cone Vase on page 76 and
the Raindrop Vase (opposite), make this Bud Vase out of black
self-hardening clay, then varnish once it's dry (see page 40).

LAMP

1 Shape the clay into 0.4" thick coils by rolling them out on the workbench. You can make them as you shape the lamp or prepare them in advance and keep them under a damp cloth. Wrap a coil around itself in the center of the banding wheel, giving it an oblong snail shape, and squeeze the rows together tightly.

2 When you have the size you want for the base of your lamp, cut away the excess coil with a knife. Stick the coils together by pinching them with your thumb and forefinger, then stretching them from outside to inside with your finger. Turn the clay slab over and do the same on the other side.

3 Place the first two coils around the edge of the clay disc and cut off the excess with a knife. Join the two ends of the coil by applying pressure with your fingers.

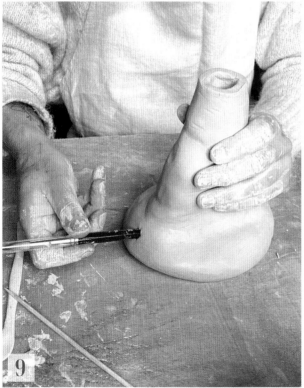

4 With the flat part of the sculpting tool's pointed end, join the outer seams from the bottom of the piece to the top.

5 Using a round-ended sculpting tool, smooth the coil seams on the inside of the lamp.

6 Place new, smaller coils on top, narrowing the opening and joining them as you go.

7 Place three new rows of coils on the lamp, maintaining the size of the opening. Join the two ends of the coils by applying pressure with your fingers.

8 With the flat part of the sculpting tool's pointed end, join the outer seams from the bottom of the piece to the top, then from top to bottom. Smooth the piece with wet palms, rotating it on the banding wheel to make sure all small imperfections are gone. Also check its alignment: if the neck isn't completely centered, place your hands flat on either side of the lamp and straighten it slightly.

9 Make a hole in the bottom of the lamp using a wooden skewer and enlarge it using the handle of a paintbrush. The hole should allow an electrical cable to pass through once the lamp is completely dry. The self-hardening clay shrinks as it dries, so make the hole bigger than the diameter of the electrical cable.

10 Once the piece is dry, apply a coat of gesso and allow to dry for 30 minutes. Then apply two coats of gray acrylic paint over the whole piece, letting it dry for 30 minutes between each coat. Using a small brush, paint a vertical line in gold acrylic paint (see page 180). Leave it to dry, then fit the lamp's electrics.

DRIP PAINT VASES

Using the same technique as the Cone Vase on page 76, make this
set of vases in grey self-hardening clay. Once they're dry, paint the
tops, allowing the paint to run down the sides (see page 180).

TWO-TONE VASE SET

Using the same technique as the Cone Vase on page 76 and the Collared Pot on the next page, make this set of vases out of red self-hardening clay, then varnish the top halves (see page 40).

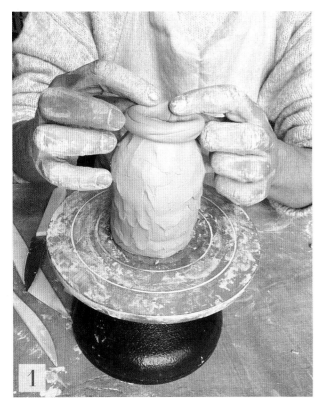

COLLARED POT

1 To flare out a container's opening, add larger coils. Place the first one around the neck and join the two coil ends by applying pressure with your fingers.

2 With the flat part of the sculpting tool's pointed end, join the outer seams from the bottom of the piece to the top.

3 Using a round-ended sculpting tool, smooth the coil seams on the inside of the vase.

4 Place a second larger coil around the neck and join the two coil ends by applying pressure with your fingers.

5 As before, seal the outside seams using the flat side of a sculpting tool's pointed end, and the inside ones with a round-ended sculpting tool. Then smooth over the pot with a wooden or stainless-steel rib. Wet the rib, if necessary.

6 Flare out the top of the jar by gently pinching it with your fingers all around. Keep rotating the piece as you perfect the collar using your wet fingers. Work slowly to achieve an even depth around the collar.

7 Once the piece is dry, apply a coat of gesso and allow to dry for 30 minutes. Apply two coats of white acrylic paint, allowing it to dry for 30 minutes between each coat. Paint the edge of the collar gold (see page 180).

ROUND VASE

Using the same technique as the Cone Vase
on page 76, make the Round Vase out
of white self-hardening clay.

AMPHORA

Using the same technique as the Cone Vase on page 76,
make this Amphora out of red self-hardening clay
and fit the handles as described on page 26.

WIDE AMPHORA

Using the same technique as the Cone Vase on page 76,
make this Wide Amphora out of red self-hardening
clay and fit the handles as described on page 26.

SLAB BUILDING

The slab technique produces smooth, even surfaces. Working with a rolling pin and wooden batten, this technique involves assembling the different joints and parts.

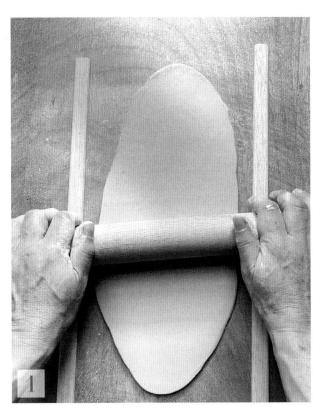

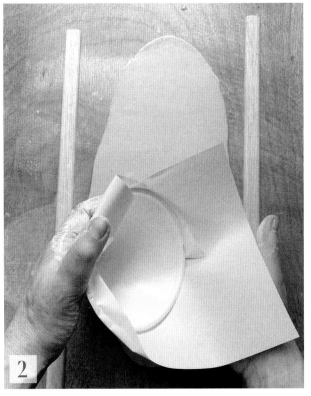

CONE-SHAPED
LANTERN

1 On your workbench, spread a ball of clay between two approximately 0.2" thick wooden battens.

2 Wrap a cone-shaped object, such as a plastic pendant light canopy, in a sheet of printing or baking paper. You can also make this lantern with a rounded shape by using a flat-bottomed bowl as a mold. If so, wrap the bowl with cling film (see page 16).

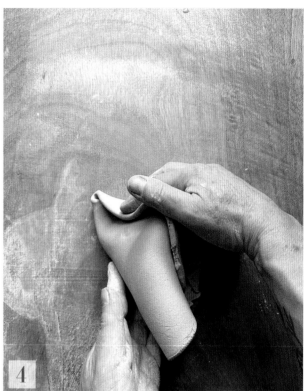

3 Place the cone on top of the clay slab and cover it completely, overlapping the edges of the clay.

4 Press along the seam with your fingers to ensure that the two layers adhere well.

5 Compress the clay along the join using a stainless-steel or wooden rib.

6 Cut away the excess clay at the bottom of the cone with a knife.

7 Place the open end of the lantern onto the workbench and smooth the entire surface with the wet rib.

8 Smooth over the entire lantern with your wet fingers to remove any imperfections.

9 Using a skewer, poke small holes in the cone, spacing them out evenly. Widen the holes a little as you go by twisting the skewer around.

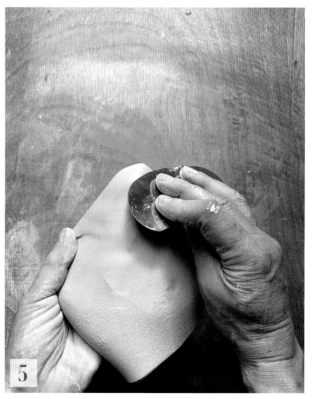

10-12 Remove the cone from the inside, starting by opening up the paper. Take out the come, then gently pull on the paper to remove it.

13 Smooth down the entire lantern once again with your wet fingers to remove any remaining imperfections, both on the inside and around the edges. If necessary, push the skewer back through the holes.

14 Use the rolling pin to roll out a ball of clay on the workbench into a disk slightly larger than the clay cone, about 0.8" larger in diameter. Use 0.2" thick battens to achieve an even thickness.

15 Smooth the clay disc using a wet stainless-steel rib and smooth out the edges with a wet index finger. To lift the slab without deforming it, use the wet stainless-steel rib.

16 Once the piece is dry, apply a coat of gesso to the cone and slab and allow it to dry for 30 minutes. Apply two coats of white acrylic paint, allowing it to dry for 30 minutes between coats (see page 180), then varnish the whole piece (see page 40).

EGG DISH

Using the same technique as the Cone-Shaped Lantern on page 100, make the egg dish out of white self-hardening clay, then paint and glaze it (see pages 180 and 40).

DISPLAY PLAQUES

Instructions on page 108.

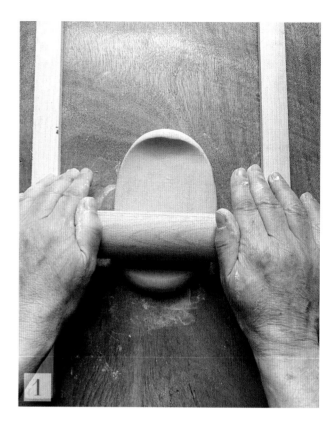

DISPLAY PLAQUES

1 On your workbench, roll out a ball of clay between two approximately 0.2" thick wooden battens.

2 Turn the slab 90° to form a round shape. If you keep extending the clay in the same direction, you will create an oval-shaped plaque.

3 Using a round cookie cutter with a diameter of about 0.4", punch a hole in the top of the plaque.

4 & 5 Smooth the edges of the plaque with a wet index finger and the surface with a wet stainless-steel rib.

6 To lift the plaque without deforming it, use the wet stainless-steel rib.

7 Once the piece is dry, apply a coat of gesso and allow to dry for 30 minutes. Apply two coats of white acrylic paint to the plaque, allowing it to dry for 30 minutes between each coat (see page 180). Varnish the plaque (see page 40) and attach a small string through the hole.

CUTTING BOARD

Using the same technique as for the Display Plaques on page 107, make the Cutting Board out of white self-hardening clay, then paint and varnish it (see pages 180 and 40).

DEEP RECTANGULAR DISH

Instructions on page 112.

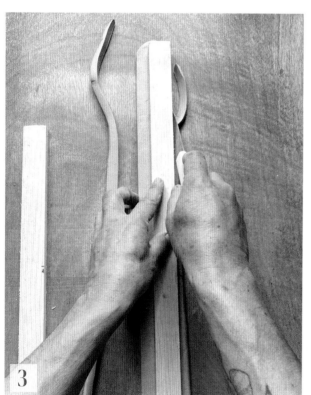

DEEP RECTANGULAR DISH

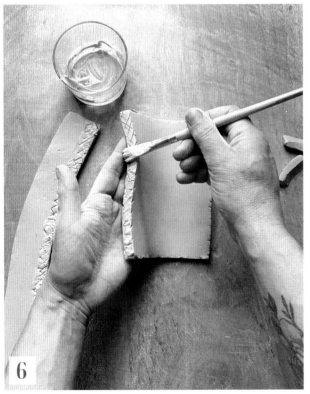

1 On your workbench, roll out a ball of clay between two wooden battens about 0.3" thick, then cut out a rectangle using a set square and knife.

2 Make a long sausage between your fingers and place it between the battens. Flatten the sausage with the roller to make a ribbon with a length that is twice the width of the rectangle + twice its length + 0.8".

3 Using a knife and a wooden batten, cut this strip so that it is 1.6" wide.

4 Cut off the ends at right angles using the knife and a wooden batten.

5 Hatch (see page 26) a 0.4" strip down edge of the ribbon using a knife or potter's pin tool. Also, hatch the edges of the slab.

6 Apply slip to all hatched areas using a brush (see page 26).

7 Place the clay ribbon around the slab and trim as required. Also apply slip to the two short connecting ends of the side strip.

8 Roll out a small clay coil, about 0.2" in diameter, by hand and place it around the inside seam between the bottom slab and the side strip. Press the coil with your index finger all the way around to make it stick.

9 Use the round end of a sculpting tool to smooth the coil all the way around and finish with a wet index finger.

10 Seal the side strip connection point using the sculpting tool, in this order: inside, outside, and then on top.

11 Smooth the entire surface of the dish with wet fingers to remove any imperfections.

12 Cut two strips that are 4.3" long and 0.4" wide from the remaining rolled out clay. Hatch the ends of these strips, as well as the connection points on both sides of the dish. Apply slip to the hatched sections.

13 Attach the handles (see page 26) to the short sides of the dish, using the sculpting tool to flatten the edges at the connection points. Smooth over with a wet index finger and allow to dry.

CUP CANDLE HOLDERS

Using the same technique as the Deep Rectangular Dish on page 111, make these Cup Candle Holders out of white self-hardening clay and attach the handles as described on page 26.

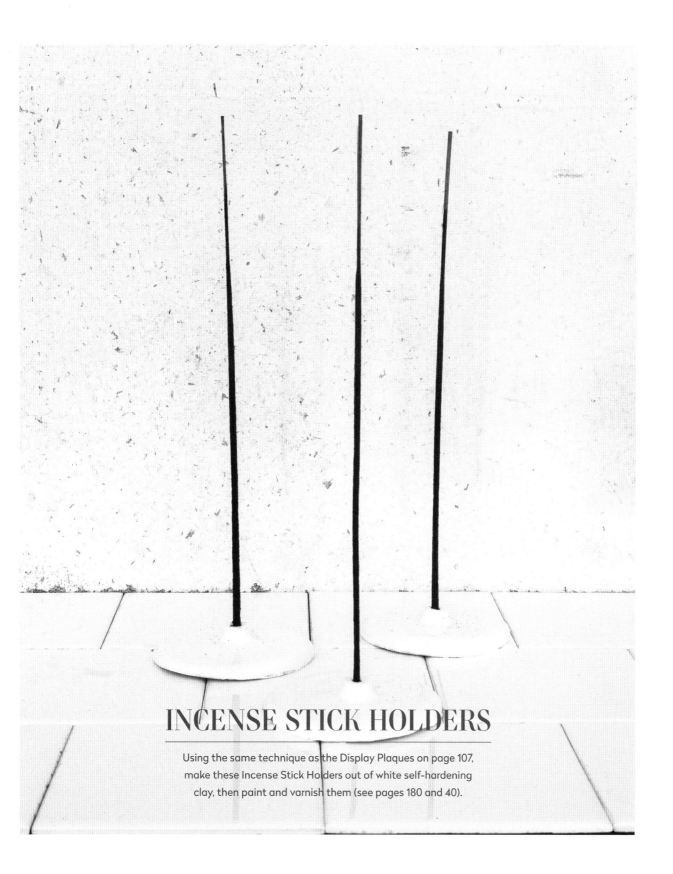

INCENSE STICK HOLDERS

Using the same technique as the Display Plaques on page 107,
make these Incense Stick Holders out of white self-hardening
clay, then paint and varnish them (see pages 180 and 40).

STAR GARLAND

1 On your workbench, roll out a ball of clay between two approximately 0.1" thick wooden battens. Cut out a dozen stars using a clay cutter.

2 Punch a hole in each star using a skewer. Be careful not pierce too close to the edge to avoid weakening the hanging point.

3 Gently smooth the stars with dry or wet fingers depending on visible imperfections.

4 Once completely dry, apply a coat of gesso to some of the stars and allow it to dry for 30 minutes. Apply two coats of gold acrylic paint, allowing it to dry for 30 minutes between each coat (see page 180).

5 Arrange the gold and gray stars alternately on a piece of thin gold wire. Secure each star in place by making a small loop in the wire with pliers, just before and just after.

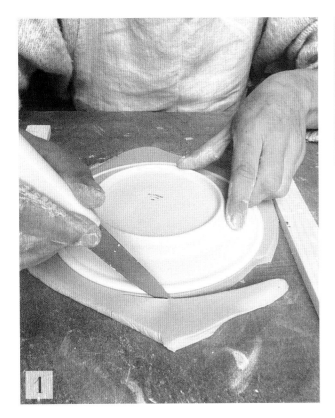

SHALLOW BOWLS

1 On your workbench, roll out a ball of clay between two approximately 0.2" thick wooden battens. Place a plate with the diameter of your choice on the clay slab and cut around it with a knife.

2 Roll a long coil about 1.2" wide on the workbench and place it between 0.3" thick battens. Flatten the coil with a rolling pin to form a strip that is slightly longer than the diameter of the clay disc.

3 Using a knife and wooden batten, cut this strip to a width of 1.2".

4 Place the strip onto the disk and check its length. If it is too long, cut it down. If it is too short, repeat step #3 with a little more clay.

5 Hatch the underside of the strip using a potter's pin tool or knife. Also hatch a 0.4" wide border around the slab.

6 Moisten the hatching with your fingers or use slip (see page 26).

7 Place the side strip onto the disc and join the ends by applying slight pressure. Also press down on the top to bond it to the slab, being careful not to distort the strip.

8 & 9 On your workbench, roll a small coil about 0.2" in diameter and place it on the inside seam between the bottom slab and the side strip. Press down on the coil with your index finger all the way around to make it stick, then smooth it out with the rounded side of a sculpting tool.

10 Seal the outer seams using the wet pointed end of a sculpting tool. Smooth with wet fingers and allow to dry.

MILK JUG & PITCHER

Using the same technique as the Shallow Bowls on page 121, make this Milk Jug and Pitcher out of white self-hardening clay and attach the handles as described on page 26.

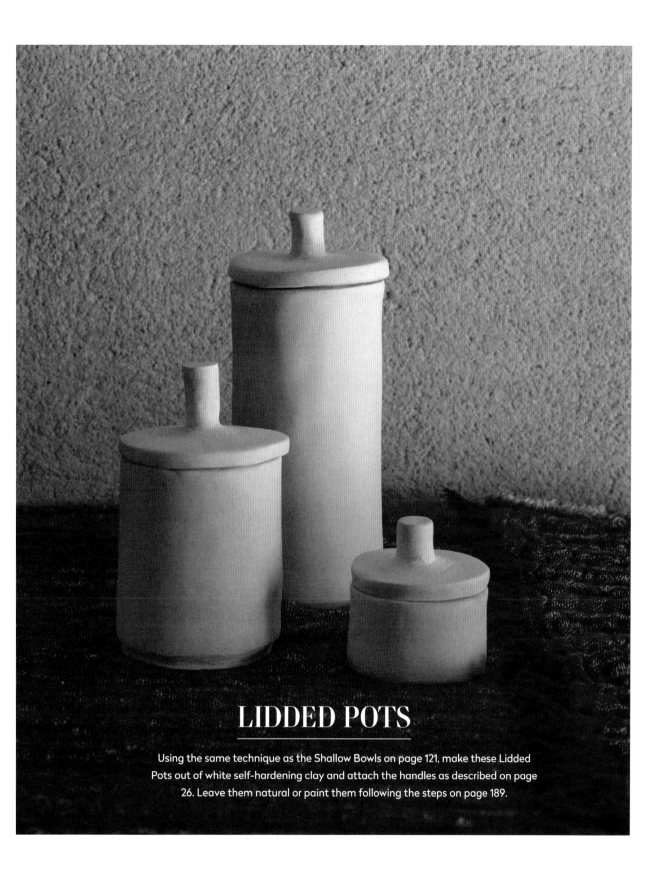

LIDDED POTS

Using the same technique as the Shallow Bowls on page 121, make these Lidded Pots out of white self-hardening clay and attach the handles as described on page 26. Leave them natural or paint them following the steps on page 189.

PRESS MOLDING

The press molding technique involves applying a slab or small pieces of clay to a mold, so that the clay takes on the shape of the mold as it dries. Press molding can be done in the hollow (inside) or the round (outside).

BOWL

1 On your workbench, roll out a ball of clay between two approximately 0.4" thick wooden battens. Cover a flat-bottomed bowl with cling film and place the clay slab on top.

2 Place your hands around the bowl and press the clay slab onto it. Press down gently on the slab with your hands, gradually working your way around the whole surface.

3 Trim the excess clay with a knife to within 0.4-0.8" from the edge of the bowl.

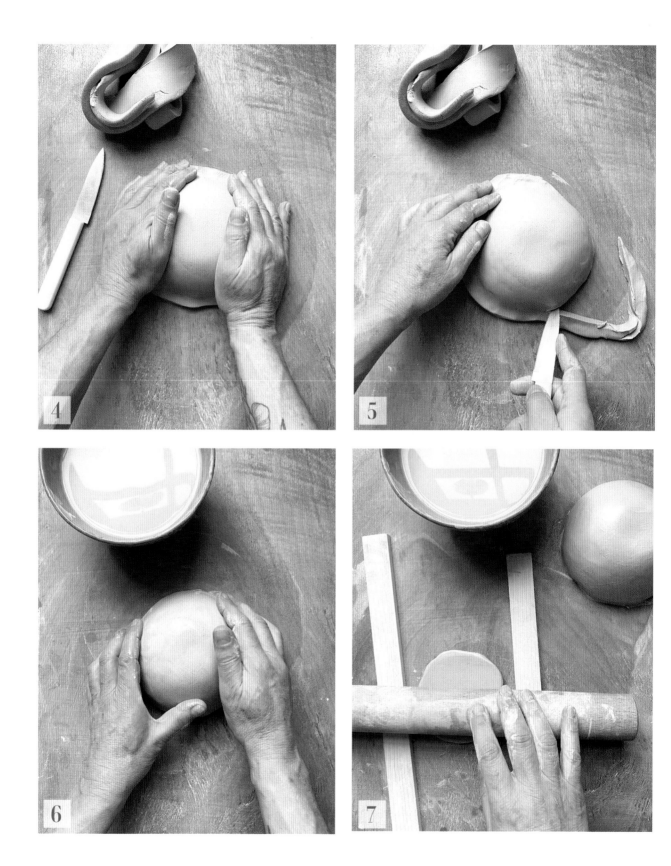

4 Reposition your hands around the bowl and continue to press the slab into the mold.

5 Trim the excess clay by running the knife along the edge of the bowl.

6 Gently smooth the entire outer surface of the bowl with wet fingers.

7 Roll out a small ball of clay on your workbench using a rolling pin and battens around 0.4" thick.

8 Using a clay cutter or glass, cut a disk out of the slab, then take another cutter or glass with a smaller diameter to make a ring about 0.8" wide.

9 With a knife or potter's pin tool, hatch one side of the ring and the bottom of the bowl where the two pieces will be joined.

10 Moisten the hatching with a wet finger or apply a little slip, then place the ring on the bottom of the bowl, making sure it is well-centered.

11 Using a wooden batten, gently tap the top of the ring so it sticks to the bottom of the bowl.

12 On your workbench, roll a thin coil about 0.2" in diameter and place it on the inside seam between the ring and the bottom of the bowl.

13 Press down on the coil with your index finger so that it merges with the two parts to be joined.

14 Repeat steps #12 and #13, this time on the outside of what's now the base of the bowl.

15 Smooth around the outer edge of the base and the coil with a wooden sculpting tool. Use the pointed end for the outside and the round end for the inside of the base.

16 Smooth the outer and inner base seams with a wet finger. Turn the piece over and remove the bowl that was used as a mold, along with the cling film. Smooth the inside and the edge in the same way as before.

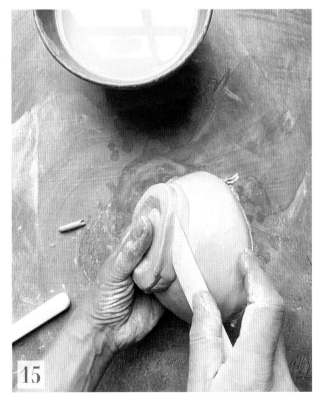

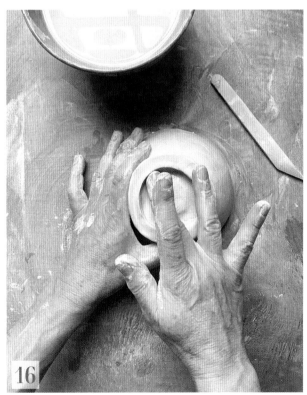

TRINKET BOWL

Instructions on page 136.

GILDED HEART VOTIVE

Instructions on page 138.

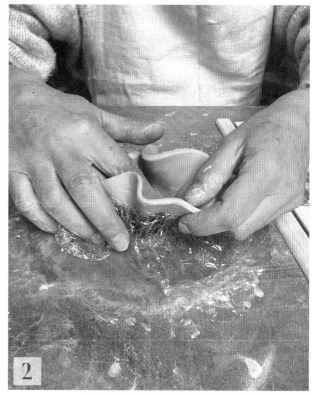

TRINKET BOWL

1 On your workbench, roll out a ball of clay between two approximately 0.2" thick wooden battens.

2 Place cling film inside a metal brioche pan. Place the slab of clay into the mold and gently lift the edges so it fits snugly inside.

3 Use your fingers to create the inner shape, especially in the hollows.

4 Run the rolling pin over the top to mark the serrated edge for easy cutting later.

5 Remove the excess clay by pressing around the outside of the mold with your fingers.

6 Remove the clay piece from the mold and then remove the cling film. Smooth with wet fingers.

7 Once the piece is dry, apply a coat of gesso and allow it to dry for 30 minutes. Apply two coats of white acrylic paint, allowing it to dry for 30 minutes between each coat (see page 180).

GILDED HEART VOTIVE

1 On your workbench, roll out a ball of clay between two approximately 0.2" thick wooden battens.

2 Cover a metal votive with cling film so you can easily peel off the clay piece later.

3 Place the clay slab on top of the ex-voto and use a rolling pin to trace the imprint.

4 Turn the slab over to the other side, so that the metal votive is on top. Press firmly with your fingers over the entire surface to fully indent the print.

5 Remove the metal votive and then remove the cling film. Sharpen the impressions using the pointed end of a wooden sculpting tool.

6 Gently shape the tips of the flames with wet fingers and smooth the edges. Remove the votive from the workbench using a wet stainless-steel rib.

7 Once the piece is dry, apply a coat of gesso and allow it to dry for 30 minutes. Apply two coats of gold acrylic paint to the plaque, allowing it to dry for 30 minutes between each coat (see page 180). To achieve an "old gold" finish, mix the gold paint with a touch of black and red acrylic paints. If you want a more brassy tone, increase the amount of black and red until you get the desired result.

IMPRESSIONS

Due to its malleability, clay lends itself particularly well to impressions. Leaves, textiles, lace, small objects, fingerprinting, pen lids, pasta, stamp rollers—the possibilities are endless!

FINGERPRINT PLATES

Instructions on page 144.

LACE PRINT PLATES

Instructions on page 146.

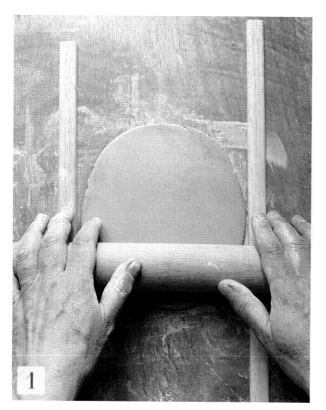

FINGERPRINT PLATES

1 On your workbench, roll out a ball of clay between two approximately 0.25" thick wooden battens.

2 Place a round container of the diameter of your choice on the slab and cut around the edges with a knife.

3 Round off the edges and smooth the top of the plate with wet fingers.

4 Make the first fingerprint in the center of the plate so you can position the others evenly.

5 Press firmly with your index finger, but not too hard. Make the other fingerprints in the same way rotating all around the central one.

6 Raise the edges of the plate upwards, slightly pleating the slab around the edges. Smooth the edges with wet fingers. Remove the plate from the workbench using a wet stainless-steel rib.

7 Once the piece is dry, apply a coat of gesso and let it dry for 30 minutes. Apply two coats of white acrylic paint, allowing it to dry for 30 minutes between each coat (see page 180), then varnish the plate (see page 40).

LACE PRINT PLATES

1 On your workbench, roll out a ball of clay between two approximately 0.2" thick wooden battens. Place a lace doily on the slab and trace the impression by pressing down firmly with a rolling pin.

2 Gently peel off the doily, checking as you go that the impression is even over the entire surface. If necessary, reposition the doily exactly in line with the impressions and run the rolling pin over any gaps.

3 Carefully peel the slab off the workbench and place it in a shallow dish. (Put cling film between the slab and the container if it's not completely smooth.)

4 Gently press the entire slab into the dish, lifting the edges and repositioning them as you go.

5 Trim the excess clay from around the edges with a knife, tilting the blade 90° in relation to the workbench.

6 Smooth the cut edges with wet fingers, avoiding running them over the impressions so as not to erase them.

7 Once the piece is dry, apply a coat of gesso and let it dry for 30 minutes. Apply two coats of white acrylic paint, allowing it to dry for 30 minutes between each coat (see page 180), then varnish the plate (see page 40).

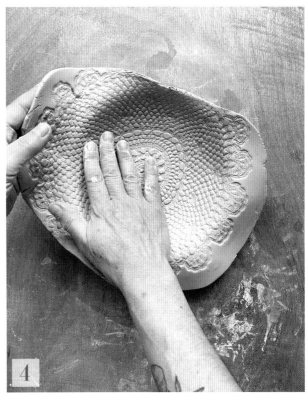

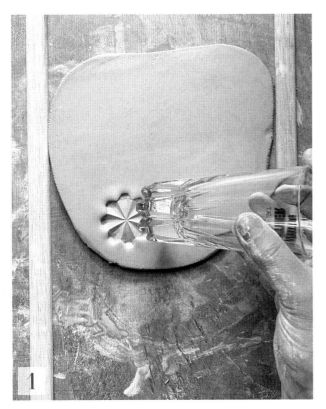

PENDANT GARLAND

1 On your workbench, roll out a ball of clay between two approximately 0.2" thick wooden battens. Stamp the slab with the bottom of a notched glass, pressing firmly but not too deep to avoid piercing the clay slab.

2 Using the top rim of the glass, cut out around the impressions.

3 Punch holes in the top and bottom of the pendants on opposite sides using a skewer or a small round clay cutter.

4 Thread a long length of linen or hemp twine through the pendant holes and secure with a single knot just before and just after.

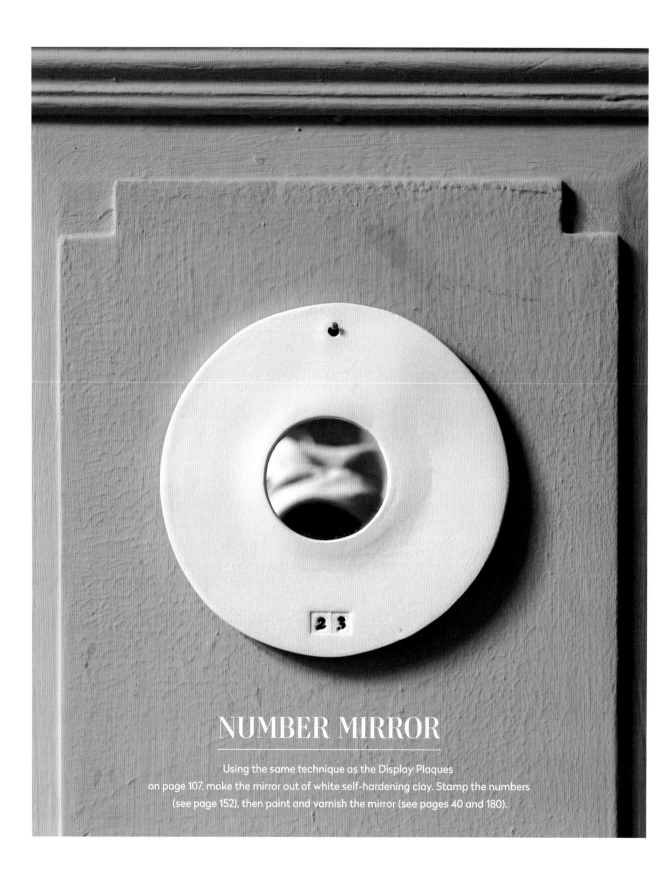

NUMBER MIRROR

Using the same technique as the Display Plaques
on page 107, make the mirror out of white self-hardening clay. Stamp the numbers
(see page 152), then paint and varnish the mirror (see pages 40 and 180).

LETTER PLATE

Instructions on page 152.

LETTER PLATE

1 On your workbench, roll out a ball of clay between two approximately 0.2" thick wooden battens. Cut out a disc of whatever diameter you like using a potter's pin tool or knife, or a plate if you want a round shape. On the workbench, roll a coil about 0.4" thick and longer than the diameter of the clay disk.

2 Place the coil around the edge of the clay disc and cut off the excess with a knife.

3 Press the coil with your index finger and thumb all the way around to make it stick to the disc. Press lightly and evenly with your fingers on both the edge of the disc and the coil.

4 Smooth the joins with dry fingers first or using a wooden rib, then again with wet fingers all the way around.

5 Gently shape the outline of the plate with wet fingers, bringing the edges upwards.

6 Use letter stamps to mark the word you want on the lower part of the plate.

7 Once the piece is dry, apply a coat of gesso and allow it to dry for 30 minutes. Then, using a small brush and colored acrylic paint, carefully fill in the impressions left by the stamps, trying not to spill over. Leave to dry for one hour, then apply two coats of acrylic paint to the whole surface using a flat brush and running it horizontally across the letters to prevent the paint from getting into the indentations. Leave it to dry for 30 minutes between each coat of paint (see page 180).

Using the base of a glass.

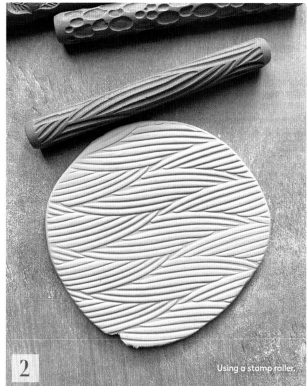

2
Using a stamp roller.

3
Using lids from pens and glue in alternating patterns.

MISCELLANEOUS
IMPRESSIONS

To create impressions, first roll a ball of clay into a slab using a rolling pin and battens of any thickness. Here are some sample ideas.

4 Using the tip of a knife to make fish scales.

5 Using a fork both horizontally and vertically.

6 Using pieces of pasta.

7 Using a key or any other small thin object.

8 Using a shell.

9 Using leaves (sage, fir, rosemary, etc.).

10 Using a spool of string at random.

11 Using a skewer to accentuate a rim.

Using a piece of hessian.

COLORING

It's essential for the self-hardening clay to be completely dry before applying paint. Additionally, acrylic or pottery paint will not adhere without gesso. However, you can also tint the clay and experiment with inlays of different materials or colors.

COLORED CLAY
& INLAYS

Unlike conventional clay—which is fired in a kiln, making it difficult, if not impossible, to incorporate materials like metal, wood or even plastic—self-hardening clay lends itself perfectly to this process. Indeed, its air-drying method avoids the unpleasant surprises caused by firing, such as splintering or cracking.

Therefore, it's possible to incorporate elements like coffee, sand, earth, wood, metal, paper, or any other material that will change the texture or develop the structure of the clay. For example, you can use metal wire or wooden rods to shape and support a piece made of self-hardening clay, which is useful for very large objects. In addition, inlaying different materials gives self-hardening clay pieces a distinctive quality that shouldn't be ignored.

Self-hardening clay can also be tinted in its natural state—i.e., before it is pinched, coiled, or dried. This technique produces different tones and textures that are achieved with conventional paint. To tint self-hardening clay, you can use powdered pigments, oil paint, or acrylic paint. Always wear gloves to protect your hands and mix them in a container to avoid staining your workbench. Only tint a small amount of clay at a time if you want to achieve bright tones, and don't be afraid to experiment with small balls of clay to avoid unpleasant surprises.

The terrazzo technique is ideal for beginners since you don't have to tint large quantities of clay. As the color is wet, take care when shaping pieces made with tinted clay to avoid smudging the colors into one another. The terrazzo technique does not work well in coiling or pinching, so it's better to stick to slab building or press molding. Don't wet your pieces during shaping, but rather sand them down once dry using fine sandpaper (120 to 180) to remove any small imperfections.

To produce an even color tone, make sure you knead the pigments or paint thoroughly into the clay. Alternatively, you can choose to make blended clay patterns, as in the "mixed earth" style, where the different shades are blended together in a visible and totally random way.

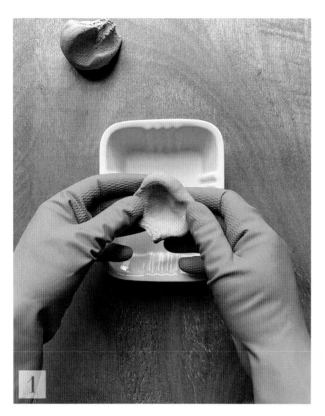

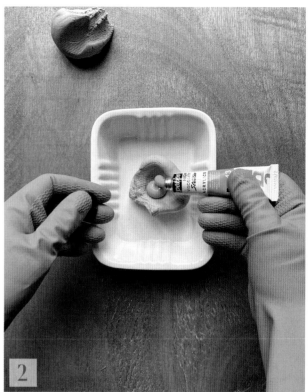

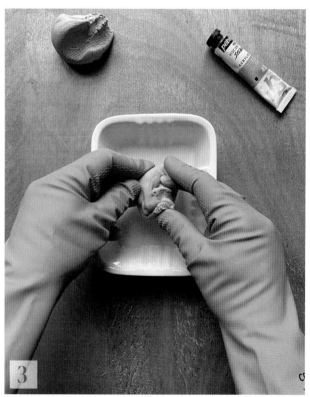

COLORED CLAY

1 Take a small ball of self-hardening clay in your gloved hands and hollow it out with your fingers to form a well.

2 Place a small amount of pigment, or acrylic or oil paint in the well. When using acrylic or oil paints, the clay will tend to become wetter. If you use too much paint, you may end up with soft, sticky clay. Work gradually, adding more paint if the tone achieved is not bright enough. If you use pigments, you will probably need to moisten the clay a bit with water.

3 - 6 Knead the clay until the paint or pigments are completely incorporated. Roll it into coils in your hands, folding them in on themselves until the paint is evenly distributed.

7 Roll the colored clay into a ball and store it in several layers of cling film to prevent it from drying out.

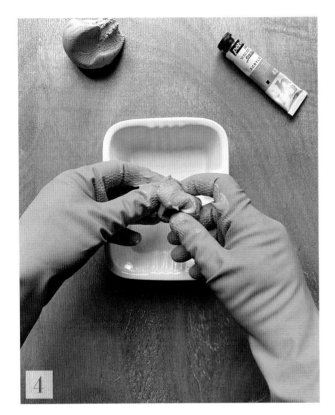

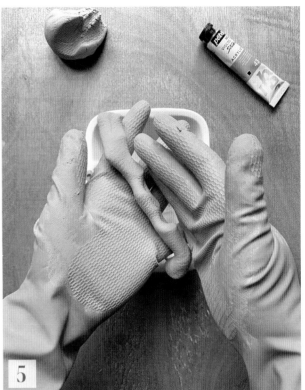

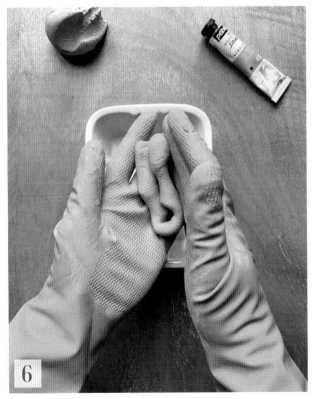

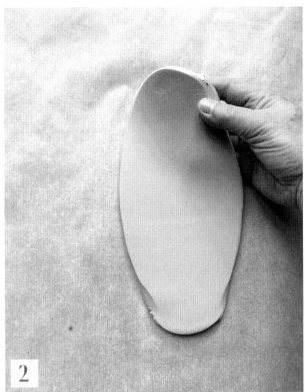

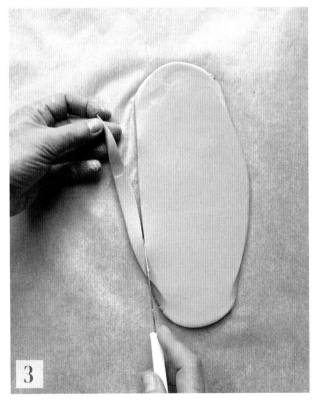

THREE-TONE
BLUE VASE

1 On your workbench, roll out a ball of clay between two approximately 0.4" thick wooden battens.

2 Arrange the clay slab carefully on a sheet of baking paper to protect your workbench, as colored clay tends to stain slightly.

3 Cut along one of the long sides with a knife to make a straight edge along which you will place colored clay coils.

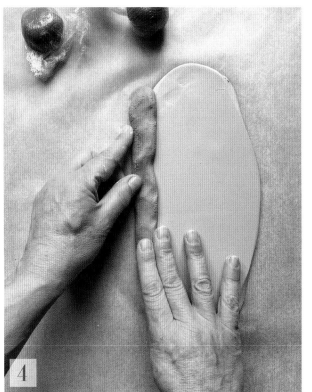

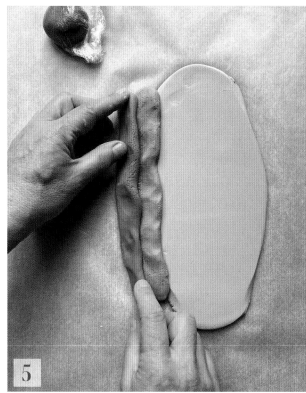

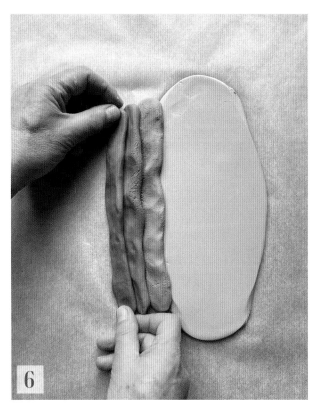

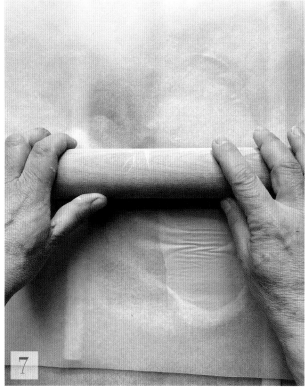

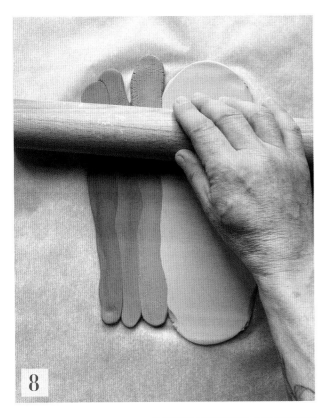

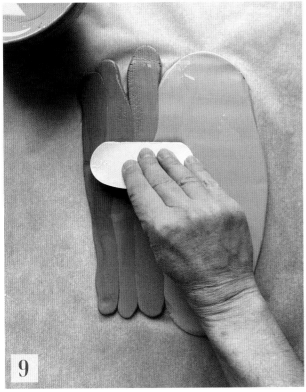

4 Place a coil of light, blue-colored clay (see page 162), overlapping the previously cut surface and press down lightly with your fingers to merge it with the white clay slab.

5 Place a coil of medium, blue-colored clay, overlapping the previous one and press lightly again to merge them.

6 Finish by placing a coil of dark, blue-colored clay, overlapping the previous one and pressing down on it once again.

7 Place battens around 0.2" thick on each side of the slab and lay a sheet of baking paper on top. Roll out the clay slab and the colored coils with a rolling pin.

8 Remove the baking paper and battens and gently roll to remove the marks and creases caused by the baking paper.

9 Smooth the whole with a slightly moistened stainless steel rib, wiping and rewetting it between each pass to prevent the colors from bleeding into each other.

10 Make the pot following the slab building instructions on page 98, then varnish it once it's completely dry (see page 40).

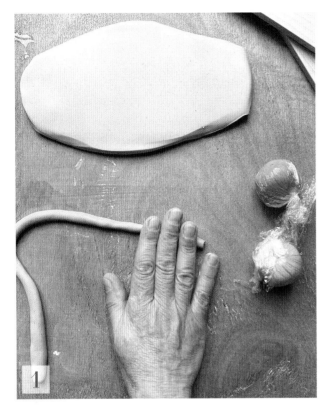

TERRAZZO COASTERS
& NAPKIN RINGS

1 On your workbench, roll out a ball of clay between two approximately 0.4" thick wooden battens. Roll small coils of colored clay.

2 With a knife, cut small pieces of clay from the colored coils, tilting the blade 45° to produce irregular triangle-shaped pieces.

3 Arrange the small colored pieces evenly over the whole surface of the white clay slab.

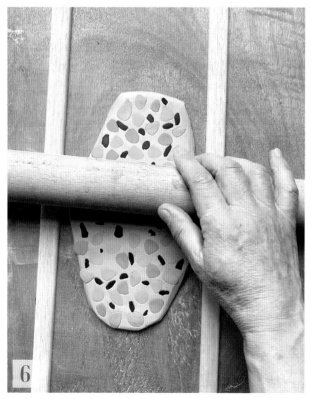

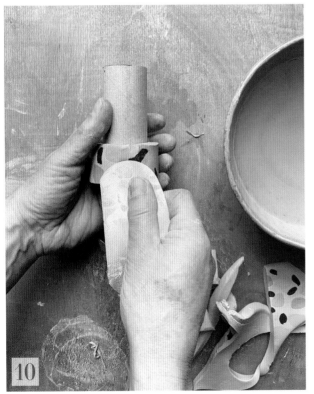

4 Press the colored pieces into place using a rolling pin.

5 Use black clay to make smaller pieces of clay and arrange them on the slab in between the other clay colors.

6 Place battens of approximately 0.2" thickness on each side of the slab and fuse the whole thing with the rolling pin.

7 Use a cookie cutter to cut out discs, smoothing the edges with your finger, but ensuring it doesn't get too wet and cause the colors to bleed into each other.

8 For the napkin ring, use a knife to cut a strip about 1.6" wide and slightly longer than a toilet paper tube.

9 Wrap this strip around the cardboard roll and press down on the seam with your fingers.

10 Seal the two ends using a stainless-steel rib, but don't wet it to avoid altering the colors. Remove the napkin ring from the cardboard roll and seal the inside seam using a wooden sculpting tool. Smooth the edges flat and place the napkin ring back on the cardboard roll.

11 Allow it to dry for 12 hours, then remove the napkin ring from the roll to prevent splitting, as the self-hardening clay shrinks when drying. Varnish the pieces once they're dry (see page 40).

TERRAZZO LAMP

1 To produce a more delicate terrazzo effect, try using a traditional kitchen grater. On your workbench, roll out a ball of clay between two approximately 0.4" thick wooden battens. Grate the different colored clays, making sure to wash the grater with soapy water after each color. If you want to achieve a terrazzo effect on only part of the slab, mask off the area you want to keep blank using baking paper.

2 Arrange the small pieces of colored clay evenly over the entire uncoated surface of the slab and place a few pieces overlapping the baking paper.

3 Roll over the colored pieces with a rolling pin in between approximately 0.2" thick battens, then remove the baking paper.

4 Make the bottom part of the lamp using the slab technique (see page 98), then the top part using the pinching technique (see page 42). Varnish the lamp once it is completely dry (see page 40) and fit the electric parts.

POLKA-DOT SOAP DISH & TOOTHBRUSH CUP

1 On your workbench, roll out a ball of clay between two approximately 0.4" thick wooden battens. Form small balls of white clay about 0.4" in diameter and place them evenly over the surface. Press down lightly on each ball with your index finger.

2 Place 0.4" thick battens on each side of the slab and roll the rolling pin over the entire surface to blend the two shades of clay together.

3 Turn the slab 45° and remove the battens. Run the roller lightly over the whole surface again to give the little white balls a round shape.

4 Make the soap dish and cup using the slab technique (see page 98). Punch a few holes in the bottom of the soap dish using a skewer. Once completely dry, varnish the cup and soap dish (see page 40).

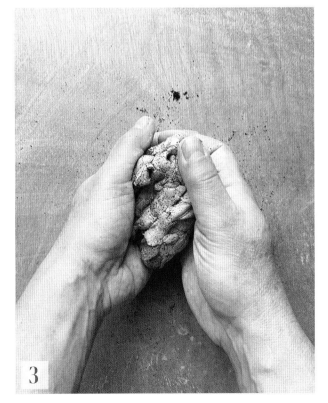

COFFEE-INLAID POTS

Inlaying is a technique that lends itself particularly well to self-hardening clay, as it's not fired in a kiln. Following the same steps described below, you can mix sand, seeds, rice, and more to create different textured effects.

1 Roll out a ball of white clay on your workbench and sprinkle ground coffee on top.

2 Fold the slab of clay in half and press down with your fingers over the entire surface.

3 Pick up the clay and press it firmly together in your hands, then knead it until the coffee powder is evenly distributed through the clay. Roll the clay into a ball and knead it again to remove any air bubbles.

4 Make the pots using the slab technique (see page 98), then glaze them once they have dried (see page 40) or leave them unglazed, depending on how they will be used.

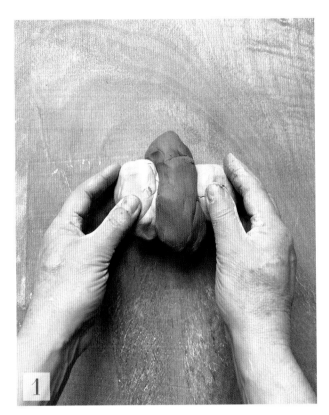

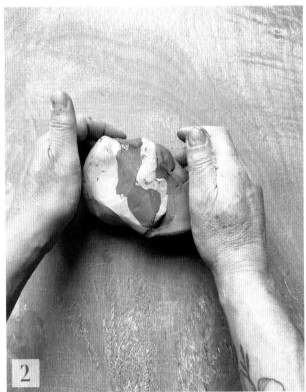

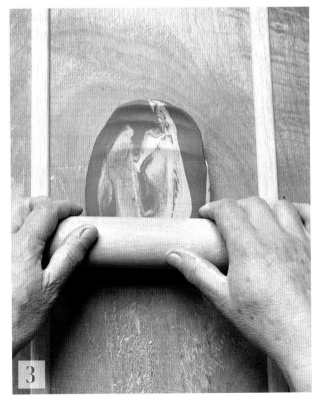

MIXED EARTH LAMP

1 & 2 To achieve a mixed earth effect, mix together two different earth shades. You can use more earth shades, but be careful to work in enough contrast to get the best result. Press together clay balls in contrasting colors. Mix the two shades of clay by hand, but don't over mix them, just blend them together. If you have experimented beforehand, you will notice that the mixtures are random and that you never get the same effect twice.

3 Roll out the ball of mixed clay on your workbench using a rolling pin and approximately 0.2" thick battens.

4 Make the bottom part of the lamp using the slab technique (see page 98), then the top part using the pinching technique (see page 42). Varnish the lamp once it's completely dry (see page 40) and fit the electric parts.

PAINTING
YOUR PIECES

Since self-hardening clay is unfired, the process of applying color is very different from that of conventional clay. Indeed, treatments like slip or enameling aren't appropriate here because these techniques require one or more firings at 2,300°F. As a result, your pieces won't be water-resistant unless you varnish or paint them. They can only be used for decorative purposes since these paints are toxic and don't comply with food standards.

To paint your pieces, choose between acrylic paint and special ceramic paint for domestic ovens. As the results are very different, you'll likely prefer one technique over the other and use it for a particular purpose. Aside from the glossy, glazed look of ceramic paint, if your pieces are going to be in contact with water, like vases, for example, you should choose no-fire ceramic paint or porcelain paint fired at 300°F. Otherwise, you can paint them with acrylic paint and varnish them afterwards to protect them from moisture.

To achieve a flawless, long-lasting result, it's essential that you apply an undercoat before coloring. For acrylic paint, apply a layer of primer, such as gesso, which will act as a filler and allow the paint to set, as well as providing a solid base. With ceramic paint, first apply a filler undercoat for the same reasons as with acrylic.

Finally, you can add a textured effect to your pieces by mixing baking soda with the gesso or acrylic paint. The amount of baking soda added to the paint depends on the look you want to achieve. The more baking soda you add, the grainier the final texture. However, be careful not to use too much so the mixture isn't too thick, as this could make it impossible to apply.

Clean your brushes with white spirit if you're using porcelain paint with 300°F firing or no-fire ceramic paint. Soapy water is sufficient for acrylic paints.

TEXTURED EFFECT

1 To achieve a lovely textured effect on your pieces, mix together gesso and household baking soda in a shallow container (see page 180).

2 Apply two coats of the mixture to the entire surface, crisscrossing the brushstrokes and allowing it to dry for one hour between coats.

Note: you can tint the gesso or mix the baking soda directly into your choice of acrylic paint.

FLOWERED PLATE & SAUCERS

Make the plate and saucers using the press molding technique (see page 126).

1 Once the pieces are dry, apply a layer of gesso and allow it to dry for 30 minutes. Begin the coloring process by painting the main motifs over the entire surface using acrylic paint. Allow it to dry for 30 minutes and, if necessary, apply a second coat.

2 Apply the background color, taking the opportunity to redraw the outlines of your motifs more clearly. Allow it to dry for 30 minutes and, if necessary, apply a second coat.

3 Finish off by painting in the details with a smaller brush. Use contrasts and place the patterns evenly over the entire surface. Leave to dry for one hour and then apply a coat of protective varnish (see page 40).

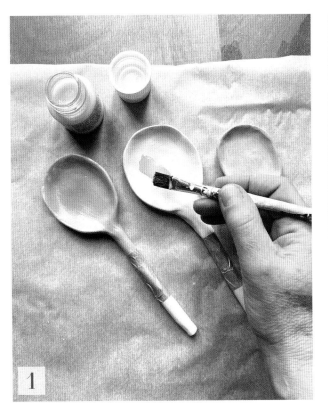

PAINTED SPOONS

Make the spoons following the steps on pages 50–53.

1 Place masking tape on the handles of the spoons to mark the area to be painted and to protect the area you want to leave unfinished. Apply an undercoat of Porcelaine 150 filler to the top part of the spoons, then leave them to dry for two hours.

2 Apply a coat of blue ceramic lacquer paint to the top part of the spoons and leave to dry for two hours. If necessary, apply a second coat.

3 Using a used toothbrush and taking care to protect the workbench, as well as your hands and the spoon handles, splatter fine droplets of black and then white ceramic paint. Leave to dry for 12 hours, then remove the masking tape.

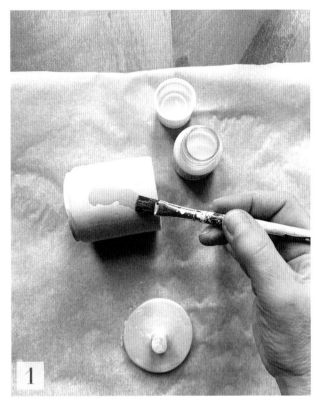

PAINTED LIDDED POTS

Make the lidded pots (see page 125) by following the slab building instructions on page 98.

1 Apply an undercoat of Porcelaine 150 filler to the entire surface of the jars, inside and out, and to the lids. Leave to dry for two hours.

2 Apply a thick coat of white Ceramic Lacquer to the lower part of the pots. Leave around 1.2" at the top unpainted.

3 Without waiting for the white paint to dry, apply a coat of blue ceramic lacquer to the unpainted part of the pot, stopping around 0.4" from the top of the white paint. Using a stiff brush, drag the blue paint down onto the white working from top to bottom. Wipe your brush as you go so you don't get white paint on the top part of the pot. Apply a coat of blue ceramic lacquer to the lids and leave to dry for 12 hours.

PAINTED POT

Apply a horizontal strip of masking tape, then apply a
coat of gesso. Apply two coats of acrylic paint. Remove
the masking tape and varnish the pot (see page 40).

CONCLUSION

Working with self-hardening clay is so easy and fun that it's almost addictive. Since the possibilities are endless, you will no doubt be tempted to immediately start a new piece while the previous one is drying. Over time, you may find that one particular technique—be it slabbing, pinching, molding, or coiling—will appeal to you more than the others, or you may in fact want to learn them all.

Moreover, once you have mastered the skills of working with self-hardening clay, you may want to start working with kiln-fired clay, sign up for a nearby workshop to perfect your skills, and, why not, even try your hand at wheel throwing! You can also work with conventional clay at home and take your pieces to a local professional for firing (for a fee, of course). As self-hardening clay isn't suitable for food containers, you will have to move on to the glazing and firing stages if you want to create dishes and containers for use in the kitchen (see page 6).

If you have children, don't hesitate to introduce them to self-hardening clay. Being non-toxic and as easy to work with as clay, they will be immediately captivated by this material. Start by showing them the simplest and most intuitive technique (pinching), then go on to teach them the press molding technique and even coiling.

Finally, take advantage of how inexpensive this material is to let your imagination run wild and create all the pieces you've ever dreamed of. It's also an opportunity to make personalized pieces in your preferred size and color. Take inspiration from the pieces in this book and adapt them to your preferences by changing their size, clay color, and more. Be sure to check out the pieces made by professional potters and ceramicists on the Internet, in galleries, at fairs, or in special stores to observe their skills and refine your own, but also to expand your creativity!

INDEX